Dreams, Culture, and the Individual

**Chandler & Sharp Series in
Cross-Cultural Themes**

GENERAL EDITOR

Douglass R. Price-Williams
  University of California, Los Angeles

CONSULTING EDITORS

L. L. Langness
Robert B. Edgerton
  both University of California, Los Angeles

Dreams, Culture, and the Individual

Carl W. O'Nell
University of Notre Dame

Chandler & Sharp Publishers, Inc.
San Francisco

Library of Congress Cataloging in Publication Data

O'Nell, Carl W   1925-
  Dreams, culture, and the individual.
  (Chandler & Sharp series in cross-cultural themes)
  Bibliography: p.
  Includes index.
  1. Dreams.   I. Title.
BF1078.053   154.6'3   76-513
ISBN 0-88316-523-6

LIBRARY OF CONGRESS CATALOG CARD NUMBER: 76-513

INTERNATIONAL STANDARD BOOK NUMBER: 0-88316-523-6

PRINTED IN THE UNITED STATES OF AMERICA

Book Design: Joseph M. Roter
Composition: Hansen & Associates Graphics

To all dream researchers
in the memory of
Dorothy Eggan

CONTENTS

PREFACE

It is an exciting undertaking to write a book on dreams. Few other such common experiences have fired the human imagination more than has the experience of dreams. As one looks into the pages of recorded history or into the accounts of the understanding of human experiences given by nonliterate peoples, one begins to gain a profound appreciation of the marvelous, and seemingly unique, contribution the dream has made to the life of man. Perhaps we shall never fully realize the depths of this contribution in bringing man to his present human status.

Man's progress can be measured by his probing into the mysteries that surround him. Even a less than perfect understanding of these mysteries often suffices to grant man some significant advantage over the conditions in which he finds himself. Despite a long history of attempts by man in various cultures to deal with the dream, the dream still largely remains a mystery. But it is a mystery which science has only recently begun to probe with any serious intent. We can feel confident that this emerging scientific interest in the dream will result in some more profound understanding of the human condition than we presently have. The real beauty of the mystery of the dream is thus to be realized. To paraphrase a statement attributed to Albert Einstein, in human experience the most beautiful thing is that which is mysterious because it is the mysterious which becomes the source of all art and science.

ACKNOWLEDGMENTS

I am grateful to many people for having stimulated my interest in dreams. The original stimulus was provided by the insight and enthusiasm of Robert A. LeVine. Among others who assisted in some material way to develop this interest were David Schneider, Calvin Hall, and Allan Rechtschaffen. In a very real, but less direct way, Dorothy Eggan provided me with the inspiration to engage in dream research.

For suggestions in obtaining materials to write this book I am grateful to Allan Rechtschaffen, Rosalind Cartwright, and the Brain Information Service, located at the University of California, Los Angeles.

I wish to thank Mr. Jack Bennett for his valuable assistance in library research. For the preparation of the manuscript, I wish to thank Arlene Kluz, Renee Kinnison, and especially Mary Grubb. Against their protests, I wish also to thank my patient family for their tolerance and understanding at those times when I was almost completely absorbed with this book.

Dreams, Culture, and the Individual

1

THE WHAT AND WHY
OF THE DREAM

The majority of human beings from all ages and all areas of the world share a curiosity about one of the most common and yet probably most fascinating of human experiences, the dream. What sort of personal experience the dream is, what it may mean for the dreamer and his group—these are among the most tantalizing questions that have occupied man from the distant past into the continuing present. Belief systems, mythologies, religions, and even sciences have been the outgrowths of attempts to answer these questions.

Most answers to the *what* and *why* of the dream have been cultural answers. That is, answers to these questions have been drawn out of shared experiences, common interpretations, and adaptive uses of the dream, facilitating adjustments in group life. Few human groups, if any, have seen fit to disregard the dream entirely, although some have minimized its significance. From historical and anthropological perspectives it seems that a majority of human cultures have attributed positive significance to the dream. A few cultures have attributed so much importance that dreams function in those cultures as a prominent and indispensable element, contributing to the welfare both of the group and the individuals in it.

Questions about dreams have nearly always been put to such specialists as practitioners in magic, religion, and the healing arts. In cultures that give science an important role in technological development, questions about dreams have come more and more to rest in the province of scientific practitioners. Western science, until recently, has not demonstrated any very affirmative position toward the study of dreams. Philosophers in Western cultures, however, have addressed themselves to questions relating to dreams. Probably the reason is the long-continued tradition of nonscientific and

1

unscientific interests in dreams; some of these interests thrive today; among them are beliefs and practices that involve astrology, witchcraft, and magic.

Within the social and behavioral sciences, psychology and anthropology have been the two disciplines most active in the study of the dream over the last century. In neither discipline, however, has the dream stood as an item of paramount interest. What we know of the dream through these disciplines has resulted largely from the work of relatively few people.

Currently, scientific interest in the dream is in ferment. The questions being asked concerning the *what* and the *why* of the dream are the same basic kinds that man has always asked. These questions, however, are being asked by more people, people who have better theories and better methods for understanding the dream than man has ever had before.

Without doubt, a great impetus to recent scientific dream study was provided by the findings of Eugene Aserinsky and Nathaniel Kleitman, studying the sleep patterns first of children, later of adults, at the University of Chicago in the early 1950s. They found that sleep has at least two distinct phases. The phases of sleep are measured by the electroencephalograph (EEG), which records patterned electrical activity in the brain. One pattern, accompanied by a rapid movement of the eyes, is called REM sleep; and the other, not accompanied by rapid eye movement, is called NREM sleep. It was soon discovered that persons awakened during REM sleep would nearly always report they were dreaming. Persons awakened during NREM sleep rarely gave reports of dream experience. Furthermore, when reported, mental experiences during NREM periods usually lacked the characteristics of fantasy that most people normally associate with dreams. It is highly probable that remembered dreams come from REM sleep, though some remembered dreams may come from NREM sleep. A study of any person's sleep and dream patterns by the EEG would reveal some differences in the dreams experienced in the two kinds of sleep periods.

These and subsequent findings suggesting that sleep patterns are multiphasic, cyclic, and apparently coordinated with distinct kinds of mental experience, promoted a conviction that the events of human dreaming are universal, patterned, predictable, and therefore considerably under the control of the experimental scientist. To some persons, at least, it seemed as though man had at last scientifically captured the dream, at least had cornered it for closer study.

These dramatic findings have proved to be a little disappointing. Man has indeed greatly extended his knowledge of the sleeping and dreaming mind. But his control of the dream even in the laboratory is not yet precise. His basic understandings of the *what* and the *why* of the dream have regrettably been put off until some future time.

The dream appears to be triggered by physiological mechanisms which are not yet well understood. As a typical person in our society you will probably not remember that you dreamed last night. But unless you were extremely ill, or under the influence of certain drugs or alcohol which interfered with the working of these physiological mechanisms, you did dream. Not only, then, is the dream universal in human experience, but it occurs also as one of the most regular and predictable of human experiences. Whether a person's dreams are well remembered, half remembered, or forgotten, these experiences occur from four to six times in a customary period of sleep, the longer the oftener.

So, if you are normal, you dream. Just how normal? The evidence is that one must literally cease functioning as a human being not to dream. It appears that only in cases of extreme brain lesion, primarily affecting the brain stem, is REM sleep with dreaming permanently suppressed.

Although physiologically triggered, the dream appears to have great psychological, social, and cultural significance. It is apparent that the dream is a complexity of diverse phenomena. Whatever else it may eventually prove to be, psychologically the dream appears to be a type of thought especially associated with REM sleep.

Scientific studies of dreams go far to contradict the idea expressed by Mercutio in Shakespeare's *Romeo and Juliet* that dreams are nothing but children of an idle brain. Some partial answers concerning the *what* and *why* of the dream have been provided by recent laboratory sleep and dream research. When it comes to questions concerning the meaning of the dream, however, scientists have not been so successful in providing answers. Generally speaking, dream researchers have found the dream to be a well organized psychological experience. It is largely on the basis of its organization that the dream is identified as thought. REM sleep is the dream state physiologically most like that of wakefulness.

Moreover, separate dreams reveal continuity in content and structure from one dream period to another in a single night. Reported dreams from an individual often demonstrate relatedness over a period of weeks and even months. The relationships between dreams for individuals have most often been demonstrated in long-term therapy, although laboratory work has supported these observations. If, psychologically speaking, an individual is the same person, asleep or awake, we may reasonably assume that dream thought also articulates with other phases of sleep and waking thought. What these articulations may be constitutes an exciting area of research on the content and meaning of reported dreams.

The dream is highly symbolic, being expressed in metaphors often obscure to the dreamers themselves. Whether we remember our dreams well or not, most of us, as adults, recognize the fantasy characteristic of dreaming. For most people, dreams are highly pictorial. The visions of the dream are usually askew from the things we perceive in wakefulness. Often the subject matter of the dream is sensuous or highly emotional and the dreamer may become deeply affected by the events of his dream. Emotions may stand in marked conflict with one another even in the same dream, so that the dreamer is often confused by his dreams.

The mode of dream thought can be so different from wakeful thought at times that some people have assumed the dream to be meaningless, or at least so far from reality as to be uninterpretable. The metaphors of our dream thought are often very different from the symbols of our wakeful thought.

Sigmund Freud, a pioneer scientist interested in dream thought, distinguished between dream *experience* or reports of such experience and the *meaning* these experiences might have in the waking thought of the dreamers. The dream as experienced or reported was called by Freud the manifest dream, or simply *manifest* content. What he considered to be the real meaning of the dream he called the latent dream, or *latent* content. In Freud's theory, the manifest content of the dream virtually always stands as a disguise of the latent content of the dream.

Many authorities, including Carl Jung, another pioneer investigating the meaning of dreams and once a friend of Freud's, have not accepted the idea that the manifest dream is simply a disguise of the latent dream. Jung felt that the symbols of the dream emerged to reveal and even clarify the depths of the dreamer's thoughts. Nevertheless, whether or not they agree with Freud, most writers on the dream find it convenient to distinguish between manifest and latent dream because the modes of dream and waking thought tend to be so different.

Physiologically and psychologically the dream seems to have a number of universal dimensions. Since man is a single species, it is not difficult to conceive reasons for this universality. Dreams occur under certain physiological conditions for virtually everyone. Dreams, typically, are expressed in metaphorical symbols earmarking the experience as dream thought.

Even some elements of manifest dream content appear to be *universal*. We may hypothesize that these elements rest on a broadly common biological inheritance and on generally common human experiences in the maintenance of life and in response to basic human social processes.

But dreams also have *particularistic* dimensions. Some of these dimensions, we may assume, rest on particularistic experiences associated with membership in a given group. These are accordingly referred to as *cultural* dimensions. Yet within any particular human group people have special experiences associated with their being male or female, young or old. Added to all of this, of course, is that fact that each individual has certain unique life experiences not shared by others. Each individual learns unique things and develops a unique personality, the uniqueness of which is reflected in dream thought.

Two particularistic dimensions frequently of interest to dream investigators have been indications of cultural or group membership and male/

female distinctions. It may be an interesting exercise to attempt identifying the cultural and sex identities of the persons whose dreams are recounted here. The reports are from young people of approximately the same age. The contributors are both male and female, three of them being residents of a large city in Midwestern United States, and three of them being Zapotec Indians from Southern Mexico. The Zapotecs are primarily an agricultural people with a rural way of life. Zapotecs of both sexes begin to assume adult obligations at a younger age than is customary for young people in American culture.

The six reported dreams follow.

1.   In my dream I encountered a man with a very dark skin who said: "I am going to eat you up," and I saw his hands reaching out to grasp me! I felt that my own hands also were very long. His face was very ugly. Then my husband said: "How can they say that the devil does not exist? And we left the baby at home!" We immediately went back home, running. I woke up then and found out that it was only a dream.

2.   I dreamed that there was a *jaripeo* (bull-baiting contest) in the town of San Juan. Some men were fighting and I was in the middle of those men. I felt that all of my teeth fell out. I told one of those men: "Look what you have done to me. I am going to sue you." Then I went into the corral and began teasing the bull. I seemed to have great advantage over him. I fought out that bull, known as the *barroso* bull, after only two movements!

3.   I dreamed I got married and went away to live in a big house. I had lots of money and gave my brother some. I also bought him a house and a car. Then I killed my husband for something he did, similar to something my father did. I fell in love with a handsome man but soon came to hate him. Then I went to California where I bought pretty clothes and lived in a house with a mink-covered room and a very large swimming pool. For some reason or other I was unhappy and I woke up crying.

4.   I had a dream that as I went to bathe in a small stream, a snake became tangled around my feet. But, by getting into the water I was able to get free of the snake. Then a big hail storm came up and it injured my head. It seemed to me that I died there.

5.   Before I went to sleep, I was thinking of a girl named Debbie and a friend named Van. Then I dreamed about them—I dreamed we were riding around in the 1940 Ford coupe my dad got me. First, we were walking to the car. The car hadn't been started all winter and we thought the battery was dead. Van, my buddy, turned the key and the car started up. I remember the fun we had going around icy corners very fast.

After awhile we got out of the car and Van went home. Debbie came to my house for a coke. Nobody was home. For some reason she started to undress. Then I woke up.

6.   Once I dreamed that I was in the jungle where the scenery was dark and gloomy. I walked slowly but all of a sudden I saw a long silvery snake. I screamed and ran but when I ran I fell into a hole with five or six large and ugly snakes in it. I just stood there in silence, slowly dying inside. One of the large snakes struck at me suddenly and I woke up.

In identifying the dreamers by culture and sex, you are correct if you said that number 1 was dreamed by a Zapotec girl, number 2 by a Zapotec boy. Number 3 was dreamed by an American girl and number 5 by an American boy. Dreams numbered 4 and 6 probably caused you some difficulty because in the set of six reports they are least revealing of manifest dream elements which help us recognize the cultural and sex identities of the people who reported them. Actually, dream 4 was reported by a Zapotec boy and dream 6 was reported by an American girl.

Dreams 4 and 6 are dreams which might be reported by anyone regardless of sex or culture. Manifest dream elements such as serpents, death, storms and water are frequent elements in human dreams everywhere. When they constitute a dominant part of a dream theme, they serve as examples of what has been referred to above as dream universals. There are many such elements in reported dreams. While their appearances in dreams are universal, we cannot yet safely make the assumption that these common elements are universal in meaning.

With dreams 1, 2, 3, and 5, you probably found it easier to identify the sex of the dreamers than the culture of the dreamers. The girls' references to husbands, for example, clearly distinguished these dreams from those of the boys. In comparing the girls' dreams, certain items of manifest cultural content help us distinguish between the dreams of the American and Zapotec girls. The cultural items of bull baiting and the Ford car supply us with important clues for distinguishing cultural affiliation in the boys' dreams.

Taken as a set, the six dreams provide us with a reasonably good sample of manifest dream thought, illustrating that the symbols and logic of dream thought are in a mode different from that of waking thought. Appraised by the logic of wakefulness, each dream is tinged with qualities of the unexpected, the contradictory, the grotesque, the improbable, the magical. We have in the Zapotec girl's dream her diabolical vision and a perception of an unnatural length in her own hands; the inexplicable skill in playing out a dangerous bull in the Zapotec boy's dream. There are the fantastic riches and magical activities of the American girl in her dream, and the highly improbable performances of both car and girl friend in the American boy's dream. There are weirdly illusional characteristics in the contents of dreams 4 and 6, including the dreamers' sensations of dying in both dreams, which clearly place these reports in the realm of fantasy.

2

DIMENSIONS OF DIFFERENCES
IN DREAM CONTENT

This chapter is devoted to a discussion of differences which appear in dreams. Most studies of differences in dreams have been done along the dimensions of sex, age, and cultural affiliation.

For the social or behavioral scientist interested in studying differences in the dreams of people grouped by sex, age, and culture, the most rewarding area for study is that of the manifest content of dreams. Empirically, the manifest content of dreams has been found to be variable along these dimensions. More and more scientists from the various disciplines interested in the dream have come to endorse the utility of manifest-dream analysis in recent years. The consensus among these various scientists is that the manifest level of dream content, potentially, can reveal much to us concerning the dream and what it reflects of the dreamer and his life situation.

Among psychologists, Gardner Murphy has been instrumental in directing the attention of other scientists to the importance of dream study. Murphy's influence has extended to many people, not alone psychologists, interested in manifest-dream analysis. Murphy maintains that the dream is perhaps the richest source of psychological material to which we have access for uncovering the form and content of individual personality. Since the publication of his book *Personality*, which appeared almost thirty years ago, Murphy has argued for a greater use of dream content in the study of individual personality differences.

Perhaps the leading exponent of manifest-content analysis in psychology is Calvin Hall. Since the 1950s, he and his many associates have collected and analyzed literally tens of thousands of dreams in an effort to derive meaningful categories of manifest content. These categories and a method of analysis

7

developed with them have been applied to the understanding of sex, age, cultural, and other group differences among people in various life situations. In the light of their extensive analyses of the dreams of many groups of people, Hall and his associate Vernon Nordby in a 1972 volume, *The Individual and His Dreams,* indicate how an individual might attain a deeper understanding of himself through using their method of manifest-dream analysis.

Among anthropologists interested in the study of the cultural dimensions of dreaming through manifest-dream analysis, the names of George Devereux, David Schneider, and Dorothy Eggan are prominent.

Being a psychoanalyst as well as an anthropologist, Devereux has a strong orientation toward Freudian dream theory. Nevertheless, he has been more flexible than many Freudians in analyzing the dreams of people in other cultures. An important aspect of this flexibility has been his acceptance of the manifest content of dreams as being important in itself and not simply a means to get at latent content. In an intensive analysis of the dreams of a patient in an American Indian culture, to which Devereux applies the pseudonym Wolf Culture, Devereux uses a manifest-content analysis of the dreams with great success in attaining a deep understanding of both his patient and the culture.

David Schneider applied manifest-content analysis to the dreams of the Yir Yoront, a cultural group of Australian Aborigines. Although his analysis of manifest content was limited to four areas: aggression, death, sexual intercourse, and the presence of white culture, Schneider found that manifest-dream themes reflected important values and other elements in the culture of his dreamers. Aggressive and sexual acts in the dreams of the Aborigines reflected in a parallel way both permitted and tabooed behavioral expectations in Yir Yoront culture.

Among anthropologists, Dorothy Eggan was most outspoken in advocating manifest-dream analyses to get at not only the cultural differences but also the personality differences between peoples. Her work among the Hopi, an Indian group of the American Southwest, stands as a monument of her dedication to this particular area of research. Although Eggan clearly perceived problems in developing the methodology of manifest-dream analysis, she perceived these problems to be in the nature of a challenge to the social sciences. She advocated the concerted effort of dedicated scientists working cooperatively to meet the difficulties of the challenge.

Sex-Related Differences

Some differences have nearly always been found in the manifest content of the dreams of males and females in any culture in which such dreams have been studied in detail. We should expect to find such differences if dream experience relates to wakeful experience. Not only are there important anatomical and physiological differences between the sexes, but cultures also typically elaborate these differences so that some distinctions are customarily made between male and female roles in all areas of life. Differences in male/female dreams often can be accounted for in the light of differences in waking-life experiences.

Among the more important divisions of manifest content to be found in dreams is the general category of dream characters, according to Calvin Hall. Adult male/female dreamers in American culture manifest some interesting differences in the characters which appear in their dreams. More characters appear in women's dreams than in men's dreams. There are roughly equal percentages of male/female human characters in the dreams of women; male human characters appear in a ratio of almost two to one in men's dreams. Occupational and vocational characteristics of the characters are also often more explicit in the dreams of males than they are in the dreams of females. As compared with men, women tend to recognize more of their dream characters as acquaintances or persons known to them in wakefulness.

Animal characters are important in dreams, and they appear with about equal frequencies in the dreams of adult men and women, according to Robert Van de Castle, a psychologist, who has studied the manifest content of thousands of dreams, and who, along with Calvin Hall has written an important work on the manifest-content analysis of dreams.

The types of animals dreamed about are somewhat different between the sexes, however. Women tend to dream more of mammals, while men tend to dream more of nonmammals, especially birds. Reptiles from snakes to dragons figure more prominently in the dreams of men than they do in the dreams of women.

But, returning to human characters, babies figure more prominently in women's dreams than in men's dreams. For women, babies and children are more frequently in their dreams at times of menses and during pregnancy. Typically, dreams of babies and children increase steadily over the period of the pregnancy, usually coming to their highest frequency about the time of delivery.

Characters which appear in dreams are usually most important for the types of interactions in which they engage. Even though there are more characters in their dreams, women dreamers interact less often and less intensely with these characters than do men dreamers. In their dreams, women tend to be receivers; men in theirs tend to be doers. Of the types of interactions encountered between dream characters and dreamers, women dreamers are generally supportive, neutral, or ambivalent to others. Men dreamers engage more in active interactions, often of an aggressive or sexual nature.

If all types of encounters are considered, males are considerably more active in their dreams than are females. Interestingly, males are both more aggressive and more friendly to others in their dreams simply because they are more active. Controlling the level of activity expressed in dreams, and comparing friendly with aggressive encounters, it appears that female dreamers may be a bit more friendly than male dreamers. In their dream friendliness, males are more friendly to female characters, less friendly to male characters.

Aggression of one sort or another is frequent in the dreams of both males and females. Dreamers of both sexes are more frequently the recipients of aggression from other dream characters than they are the initiators. Physical aggression is the more common for men dreamers; verbal aggressions and emotional dispositions to aggression are the more common for women dreamers.

Manifest sexuality is less frequent than manifest aggression in dreams of both males and females. Mixed aggressive sexual content is not infrequent for mature persons of either sex. Male dreamers dream more frequently of sexual encounters with unknown persons than do female dreamers, who interact sexually more frequently with dream characters known to them in waking life.

The frequency of manifest sex dreams is extremely variable from one person to another, and so is the variety of sex acts in dream content. The variety of sexual interactions in dreams tends to be much greater than the dreamer is likely to experience in waking life. The sexual dreams of physically mature males may be accompanied by nocturnal emissions. But nocturnal emissions do not accompany all the sex dreams of males. Occasionally, dreams are reported as occurring with nocturnal emissions even when the manifest content of the dream is not sexual. Laboratory studies have revealed the fact that tumescence of the penis is a fairly common physiological occurrence in males during REM sleep whether the content of the dream is sexual or not. Some nocturnal emissions may be triggered by a physiological mechanism not matched by a psychological counterpart in dream experience.

Virtually absent in dreams recorded in the laboratory, the experience of nocturnal emission is commonly reported in home dreams. Laboratory studies indicate that when dreams are collected from normal subjects of either sex by an experimenter of the opposite sex, the sexual content of reported dreams tends to be greater than when subjects are reporting dreams to an experimenter of the same sex.

The dream settings of women are more definitely bounded than are those of men. Women report dreaming of being inside buildings or enclosures. Often the dreams of women are in houses or other types of dwellings. Men's dreams are more frequently set in open spaces, often open country. Women also tend to dream more often of familiar physical surroundings than do men.

Number and size typically are used to define things appearing in the dreams of men. Qualitative elements, texture, and often color are characteristics of things which appear to be important in the dreams of women. Women are more evaluative and emotionally expressive than are men in their manifest dream experiences.

In an unreported study conducted several years ago in which I collected dreams from a select sample of male and female high-school students in Chicago, my findings in the analysis of dream content were in essential agreement with the findings of other investigators. Part of the study involved attitudes of dreamers toward their dreams and sleep.

The majority of both boys and girls indicated a liking for sleep. Boys were somewhat less positive than girls in their attitudes toward sleep. While the attitudes of both girls and boys were more frequently positive toward sleep than toward dreaming itself, about three-fourths of both sexes gave some indication of a liking for their dreams.

Girls more frequently than boys gave answers indicative of an awareness of dreaming. Girls also more frequently gave answers indicative of discussing their dream experiences with others. Almost 94 percent of girls as opposed to 78 percent of boys indicated that they sometimes talked over their dream experiences with other people. Girls are more in the habit than are boys of often telling dreams to others; 45 percent of girls as compared to 21 percent of boys indicated that they often told their dream experiences to others.

Studies of dreams of school children in the 1930s, as well as more recent work, indicate sex-related differences in dream content for children. Jersild and his associates noted differences in the dreams of American school children from five to twelve years of age. From a backdrop of research done on the manifest content of adult dreams, sex-related differences in the dreams of children are interesting because they appear to relate in general to differences found in adulthood.

Boys tend to lead girls in having dreams in which the manifest content relates to the possession of desirable goods, travel and diversion, having successful fights with others and devising ways of escaping dangers, falling, being involved in accidents, receiving injuries, and engaging in violent and active behaviors. Girls, on the other hand, tend to lead boys in having dreams in which the manifest content relates to the dreamer's friendly associations with relatives and friends and the loss of such loved ones, of altruism, of getting married or becoming a parent, of being helped by magical solutions to problems, of being threatened, and of becoming poor. Girls, more than boys, tend to have dreams connected with everyday events, and of persons and objects in their waking lives. Even at a young age, boys tend to remember their dreams less well than girls. Boys appear also to respond less positively to their dreams, to state a liking for their dreams, than do girls.

With caution, it seems that we can draw some tentative conclusions about sex-related differences in dreams. Some of the differences appear to extend from childhood into adulthood. Even in cases where dream differences are slight, they are consistent and often form a general pattern with more obvious waking-life differences. Most dream differences appear to be related to differential cultural expectations for males and females in the world of wakefulness. Rarely does there appear to be a one-to-one correspondence between manifest-dream experience and waking-life experience. Let us remember here the assumption that dream thought is qualitatively different from wakeful thought. Nevertheless, the dream seems to go a long way in reflecting conditions in waking life, particularly as these relate to some of the more basic and personal needs of dreamers.

Just as the waking social lives of males and females in our culture are somewhat different from one another, so are the manifest contents of their dream experiences different from one another. The kinds of dream characters males and females dream about and the possible kinds of social interactions these characters have with the dreamer and one another in waking life are reflected rather interestingly in their dreams. To take one of the more obvious examples, the greater preoccupation by females with babies and children in their dreams is certainly a reflection not only of biological but also of social differences between the sexes. The fact that dreams with manifest content relating to babies and children increase at the times of menstruation and pregnancy for females reveals some avenue of continuity between wakefulness and the dream. The young girl, too, reveals something of the nature of the impending expectations of her sex role in her more frequent dreams of marriage and parenthood, which in our culture are more central for girls than for boys.

The greater aggressiveness on the part of male dreamers also reflects expectations positively endorsed by the culture. Yet males—as husbands, fathers, friends, and lovers—are expected to be supportive and friendly, and this expectation too is well expressed in dream content. The generally higher level of physical activity attributed to males in wakefulness is also clearly expressed in manifest dream content. The different ways dreamers have of identifying their dream characters seem not to be far removed from the different ways in which people are identified and dealt with by the sexes in waking life. Men often recognize and relate to others in wakefulness primarily on a basis of occupation. Women, on the other hand, and particularly if they are not engaged in work outside the home, are culturally freer to relate to others in more personal evaluative ways.

Our culture has seemingly also been somewhat more tolerant of interest in the dream by females than by males. Dreams have not been highly valued in the practical world of hard reality toward which most parents have tried to orient their sons, who will traditionally become the breadwinners of families. The male/female differences in this respect may be reflected in adolescent attitudes toward sleep and dreaming and in the differing ease and frequency with which the two discuss their dreams with others.

Age-Related Differences

If the REM period in sleep is as good an indicator of dreaming in the very young as it is in the more mature person, then children do a lot of dreaming. As much as 80 percent of sleep time in the premature infant may be REM sleep. Normally, at full term, 50 percent of a baby's sleep time will be spent in REM sleep. By two years of age this is reduced to about 30 percent. Further but gradual reduction in REM time occurs until early adulthood, when it constitutes about 20 to 25 percent of sleep. The amount of REM sleep a person experiences stabilizes somewhat in adulthood, so that even in old age a person may not experience much less REM time than he did in his early adult years.

When we look at age as a primary factor affecting the content of dreams, age appears to be not as important as sex. But this is not to say that in dreams there are no differences related to age. Many of the age-related differences which have been observed may indeed be very important differences. Relatively less attention has been paid to the dreams of the very young and the very old than has been paid to the dreams of those in intermediate age groupings.

Just as a person begins in early childhood to develop his personality which endures, although modified, into his adult years, it seems that in childhood one may develop a style of dreaming which persists into maturity. Similarly, a person's own personal "dream language"—the metaphors and logic of his dream thought—may be developed simplistically in childhood, only to be elaborated with aging. The similarities and consistencies perceived in a person's dreams over a period of years may be due not only to the dream being a reflection of a person's basic adjustments to life but also to the language one has developed to express his dream thoughts.

In general, young children's dreams appear to be simpler and more straightforward than the dreams of adults. The manifest contents of a young child's dreams often clearly express his wants and fears as these are also expressed in waking life. Thematic material is typically less complex in the dreams of children than in the dreams of adults. The greater candor of the child's dream may be due, as Freud indicates, to the child's having fewer defenses in his personality structure. Without doubt, also, children's dreams are less complicated than adults' dreams because the abilities of children to think about and understand things are less highly developed. Closely related to this fact is the observation made by Jean Piaget, the noted Swiss psychologist who has studied the development of children's mental processes, that it may take a lot of physical maturation and learning before the young child is able to develop and master the complex symbolic processes associated with dreaming.

Children begin to talk about their dream experiences almost as soon as they begin to articulate speech, commonly in the second year of life. Freud, for example, in his *The Interpretation of Dreams,* discusses the dream experiences one of his daughters reported at nineteen months of age.

The content of the child's dreams seems to be restricted only by the array of experiences he may have in wakefulness. Interesting studies confirming relationships between wakeful and dream experiences have been provided by a number of investigators, including C. W. Kimmins in England, A. J. Jersild in the United States, and Jean Piaget in Switzerland.

In his study of American school children, Jersild found some topics increasing in the reported dreams of children from ages five through twelve. Such topics related to diversion and amusement, embarrassment and guilt, the loss of a loved one, and dreams of height and falling. Nightmares steadily become more numerous for children in this age bracket. With age, more pronounced increases occurred for topics related to prestige, achievement, and independence.

Certainly some of these things would seem to reflect increasing maturity on the part of the child. As a child takes on greater obligations with home and school experience, diversion and amusement become more specialized activities. Similarly, because of responsiveness to others and their expectations of him, he may have greater reason to become conscious of situations involving embarrassment or guilt. The maturing child also realistically develops a keener awareness of what it might mean for him to lose by death someone upon whom he is greatly dependent. The significance of death, its finality, and its social implications are not understood by the very young child, whereas this understanding does grow in the maturing child.

In the preteen years American children gain an understanding of independence as a social value and it becomes a goal for them. Competitive values in our culture also contribute to a striving for achievement and prestige. In the total value system these last two things are not unrelated to independence. It is not surprising that there should be an increase of these elements in children's dreams since we would expect some preoccupation with these things in wakefulness.

Not quite as easily explained are the increases in dreams of heights, falling, and nightmares. If they are interpreted as manifest elements which are symbolic of more mundane problems, then it might be possible to assume that these things symbolize striving for greater heights, possibilities of failure, and a fear of unknown experiences yet to materialize. As a child gains greater competence and knowledge he also gains the vague awareness that there are many things in his environment about which he may know little and over which he may have little control, things reflected in his nightmares.

Some dream topics, in contrast, were found to decrease in the reported dreams of children from ages five through twelve. One of these was a decline in magic as a solution to problems in the manifest dream. Also, there was a pronounced and consistent decline with increasing age in the clear inclusion of everyday events in dream experience. One is tempted to think that children, as they grow older, are less content to think of magical solutions to their problems. The tendency of older children to include less of the mundane in their manifest dreams is probable evidence of the growing complexity of children's dreams and an increasingly greater reliance on abstract symbolism not clearly related to wakeful experience.

A few manifest dream topics seem to stand out in the experience of children at certain ages. Between the ages of seven and eight, in contrast to either an earlier or a later age, children dream more of social interactions with friends and relatives and of not so friendly interactions with ghosts and goblins. Dreams of children from nine to ten in Jersild's sample also seemed to be particularly susceptible to the influences of fantasy experienced in wakefulness. The contents of stories from books, the radio, and movies made their way into the dreams of children at this age more frequently than at other ages.

What seems to be the nature of children's understanding of their dreams? What do children think their dreams are, and where do they believe the dreams originate? Piaget tells us that children go through three stages of understanding their dream experience. At first the young child sees the dream as something which both originates and occurs outside himself. He reacts to the dreams as he would to a play, to a movie, to a television program, or to a real experience actually observed. It is something produced externally which he watches. Later the child thinks of the dream as something which originates in his own head but which transpires outside himself in the immediate environment. Finally, the child comes to realize that his dreams both originate and occur totally within himself. He realizes that his sensing of the dream is completely internal to himself. Achieving this understanding of the dream, the child has developed a mature concept of the dream which makes it internal, subjective, and fictive.

Lawrence Kohlberg, an American developmental psychologist, has elaborated Piaget's methods for measuring dream concepts in the child. Studying American children and Atayal children in Formosa, Kohlberg uncovered six stages in the children's developing concepts of the dream, which are refinements of the three stages found by Piaget. Kohlberg's work, which essentially confirms what Piaget found, indicates that children pass through a fixed progression of stages before arriving at a mature concept of the origin and location of personal dream experience.

Work done with American, English, and Atayal children suggests that children achieve the same levels of dream concept at about the same chronological ages. The Atayal children appeared to be slightly behind the other children in developing these concepts.

The belief system regarding the dream in Atayal culture is that the dream may be an encounter between the dreamer and certain beings in the supernatural world. This belief may be neither well understood nor appreciated by individuals until they reach early adolescence. So Kohlberg found a rather curious situation. Children at eleven to twelve years of age had attained a mature concept of the source and nature of their dream experience. At that time, pressures for them to accommodate to the native belief system caused them to regress to a concept they held at an earlier age, one that was consistent with the cultural belief system.

Jersild and his associates found that as children mature they find an increase in the proportion of their unpleasant dreams. As a result, children develop an increasingly negative attitude toward their dream experiences. Sex differences do not appear important in this case. At ages five and six, 62 percent of the children in the Jersild sample expressed a desire to have further dream experiences; but by about age twelve 63 percent of the sample expressed the desire that they might discontinue dreaming. Positive attitudes toward their dreams, expressed as a desire to continue dreaming, had become reduced at ages seven to eight to 49 percent, to 40 percent at ages nine to ten, and to 37 percent at ages eleven to twelve.

Since in Jersild's sample older children could report dreams more easily than younger children, it was concluded that older children had more dreams. Knowing what we do now of the sleep and dream pattern, a more reasonable conclusion would be that older children are more aware of their dreams, or perhaps simply better able to report them, given their more mature experiences in general and their greater abilities to communicate these experiences.

Children's dreams have also been studied in the laboratory. David Foulkes and his associates found the manifest contents of dreams of young children, as compared to those of adults, tend to be realistic in characterization, setting, and plot. Such dreams were related, in a general way, to events and conditions in their waking lives. In some cases dreams bore demonstrable and rather specific relationships to experiences a child had had in recent daily experience or even in the presleep situation he encountered in the laboratory.

Manifest aggression which is a common element in dream content is much more common in the dreams of children than it is in the dreams of adults. Hall, for example, has found up to twice as much aggression in the manifest content of children's dreams as he has in the manifest content of adult dreams. As may be expected, this finding runs contrary to findings on the amount of manifest sexuality that appears in dreams of children and adults. Themes of a sexual nature, however, are not completely absent from the dreams of children.

Animal characters are also a commonly found element in the manifest content of dreams. As with aggressive themes, with which they may be closely associated, animals are more frequent in the dreams of children than of adults. Van de Castle found a perfect negative correlation between percentage of animal content and age in American children. As children grow older, the percentage of animals found among the characters encountered in their dreams declines precipitously. At age four, 61 percent of dream characters are animals. At age sixteen, this has declined to about 9 percent. There is still a further decline into early adulthood, when the percentage of animal characters stabilizes at about 7.5 percent.

Van de Castle also looked at the animal content of dreams relative to age in another interesting way. Using the age of menarche (the first menstrual period) as an indication of physical maturity, he hypothesized that girls who were physically more mature would have comparatively fewer animals in their dreams than girls who were less physically mature. He compared manifest animal content in the dreams of three groups of student nurses of the same age. One group, an early-maturing group, had achieved menarche by age eleven. A second group, a later-maturing group, achieved menarche at about age twelve. A third group, a late-maturing group, did not achieve menarche before age thirteen. True to Van de Castle's expectations, those in the early-maturing group had the lowest percentage of animal dreams among the three groups. Those in the second group had more animals in their dreams than did the group of early maturers. Those in group three, the least mature group, had the greatest percentage of animals in their dreams.

What is the significance of animals with respect to age differences in dream content? It has been suggested that animals are symbolic of other things in dreams, and that animal symbolism is a childlike or psychologically primitive form of symbolism. This idea helps to explain the greater frequencies of animal figures in the dreams of children as compared to the dreams of adults.

The decline of animal symbolism with age is not consistent in all cultures, a difference which suggests that cultural factors may complicate age factors in giving rise to animal symbolism. Two ideas have been used to explain these differences.

One idea has been expressed by Heinz Werner, a student of comparative mental development. Essentially, this idea is that adults in certain cultures that have simple technologies remain at a simpler level of mental development than do adults in cultures that have highly complex technologies. For example, the percentage of animal content in the dreams of adults in some American Indian cultures is higher than it is in the dreams of more technologically advanced Americans. Adults among Australian Aborigines, whose culture shows a simple level of technological development, have dreams in which about 50 percent of dream characters are animals as opposed to about 7 percent in American culture. This explanation lacks empirical anthropological support. There is no evidence from anthropological study to indicate that different cultural adaptations, which characterize modes of life for different human groups, represent biological or psychological superiority or inferiority in those groups when any two or more human cultures are compared.

The second idea has to do not with differential mental development but rather with the idea that people in different cultures develop different kinds of dream symbols to express concepts which basically may be similar. Why do people in different cultures develop different kinds of symbols? It is assumed they do so because the things with which they have contact are different. Certainly, in many technologically less advanced cultures, animals maintain a proximity and a utility to most people in daily experience which is not common in our own culture.

Certain areas of manifest content in dreams, then, change with aging. Many of the changes with aging would seem to relate to important situational factors in the lives of dreamers.

Hall and Nordby report on the dreams of a woman which were recorded over about a 53-year period. A manifest-content analysis of 600 dreams was taken for representative periods of her life from the time she was about 25 years old until she was about 75 years old.

While the dream content shows a great amount of consistency over the long period, there are important shifts in content which reveal preoccupations of the dreamer with problems in her life. Illness was a problem for her as a younger woman; content reflective of her problems with illness is more apparent in the dreams of those years. As a middle-aged woman, she felt neglected and ignored; this feeling emerged in the manifest level of her dreams in middle age. As an older woman, she achieved greater contentment with her lot in life, which showed itself in the contentment of her dreams during her last years.

Psychologists Alan Krohn and David Gutmann worked with the hypothesis that younger adults are more active than older adults, have greater control over their environment and themselves, and are more willing to confront life situations in some aggressive and decisive manner. People's changing life situations as a result of aging, it seemed to Krohn and Gutmann, should have repercussions on personality development. The psychologists postulated two basic age changes for men. Younger adult males should reveal a type of ego mastery reflective of their active, highly involved, and productive orientation to life. Older adult males should reveal a type of ego mastery reflective of a more passive, less highly involved, and more accommodating orientation to life. The manifest content of dreams was to be considered with reference to these ego-mastery orientations. Dreams were collected from Navajo males from 35 through 95 years of age. The sample was divided between younger men 35 to 54 years and older men over 55 years of age.

The analyzed dream data lent support to the hypothesis. In their dreams the younger group of Navajo males, for instance, saw themselves as more active than older Navajo males perceived themselves to be. Generally speaking, older Navajo men dreamed of themselves as more passive dream characters. Younger men tended to see themselves as central characters in their dreams, whereas older men frequently saw themselves in less important positions; some older men did not even see themselves in their dreams at all. As expected, younger males were more preoccupied than older males with work themes. Younger males dreamed of less protected situations than did older males. Younger men dreamed of being outdoors and in open spaces; older men dreamed of being indoors often in protective enclosures. Being outdoors was interpreted by the investigators as being challenging to the dreamer, possibly rendering him vulnerable to danger; being indoors was interpreted as offering security to the dreamer, giving him a less chaotic and more protective dream environment.

Culture-Related Differences

An interesting cross-cultural study making use of the manifest-content analysis of reported dreams was conducted by Robert A. LeVine, an anthropologist who worked in Nigeria. LeVine studied the dreams of male students among the Ibo, Yoruba, and Hausa, three distinct cultural groups in that African nation. LeVine's basic hypothesis was that values and motivations, differentially acquired by people as a result of being socialized into their respective cultures, will be reflected differentially by people in their dreams.

Of the three cultural groups in the study, the Ibo have a value system and a social structure that most favor the upward social mobility of its members. An individual who aspires to do so, depending on how valuable his contributions appear to the group as a result of his upward movement, can manage to achieve a great deal of upward mobility. Commensurate with this opportunity are socialization practices that encourage people to strive for individual achievement. In terms common in social science, Ibo culture sanctions high status mobility and fosters achievement motivation in its members. Yoruba culture is somewhat less supportive of status mobility and achievement motivation in its members than is Ibo culture. Of the three cultures, Hausa culture is least supportive of these things.

Theory and research both suggest that cultures that favor high individual status mobility are also those that induce the development of high levels of achievement motivation in their members. Conversely, cultures that disfavor individual status mobility are those that do not socialize their members to high levels of achievement motivation. LeVine hypothesized that achievement motivation as a psychological variable would be revealed in the manifest content of dreams. He utilized an analytic system based on the psychologist David McClelland's method of assessing achievement motivation in projected fantasy.

In line with his expectations, LeVine found that Ibo dreamers had more manifest dream content indicative of achievement motivation than did Yoruba dreamers. By the same token, Yoruba dreamers had more manifest achievement in their dreams than did Hausa dreamers.

LeVine's study did the following things: It predicted that certain cultural variables would have an influence on the development of a psychological variable called achievement motivation. He predicted that this motivational state would be unequally expressed in the three cultures he worked with. Further, it predicted that achievement motivation could be measured in the manifest content of reported dreams. Confirmation of his predictions points to the utility of using manifest dream content in the study of cultural differences.

Individual Differences

People's dreams are similar to and different from those of others not only on the basis of sex, age, and culture but also on the basis of individual experience. The magnificent intricacies and subtleties of a person's dreams reveal not only dimensions of life experience which each shares with others, but also reveal the uniqueness of each individuality. The contents of one's dreams make the dream experience one of the most personal events in one's life.

The dream has sometimes been compared to a screen on which are projected the most intimate of images; at other times, to a painting reflecting the richness in detail of deep human experience. Whatever analogies may seem appropriately applied to the dream, it is certain that whatever it is in defining one person in relation to others, the dream is also individually distinctive, at the very least as distinctive as a fingerprint.

Summary

We have explored in this chapter a very broad area dealing with differences in dreams. Studies of the differences in the manifest content of dreams have often focused on sex, age, and cultural variables. In general, these studies demonstrate that interesting and important differences between people's dreams are related to sex, age, or cultural affiliation.

3

DREAMS AND THEIR
CULTURAL SIGNIFICANCE

We take up the interesting question, in this chapter, of what dreams have meant to man in different areas of the world, in the different cultures he has produced, and at different times in his history. The dream has been humanly significant to the degree that it has had meaning for man and to the degree that he has attributed importance to its meaning.

Whatever significance man perceives in the dream, his perceptions are determined in large part by his culture. His understanding of the dream and the value, or lack of value, he attributes to the dream are basically matters of cultural interpretation. Whether man attributes significance to the dream on the basis of magic and supernatural forces or on the basis of science and natural forces, his assignment of meaning to the dream is done within the framework of his culture.

Relationship of the Dream to Wakefulness

To many early anthropologists it seemed that the preliterate peoples they studied did not clearly distinguish between the dream and wakefulness. Sir James Frazer, an early anthropologist interested in comparative beliefs in preliterate cultures, tells us in *The Golden Bough* of the Macusi Indian who dreamed that his white employer forced him to carry a heavy canoe up a series of cataracts. Suffering ill health at the time, the Indian awakened angry and reproachful at this insensitive man who had acted so inhumanely as to make his sick servant work through the night as well as the day. Apparently, the Indian considered his dream equal to wakefulness and continuous with it, to the degree that he seems to have confused his dream experience with wakeful experience.

Confusing the dream with wakefulness, however, seems not to be a common interpretation of dreams in any culture. Yet an unusually vivid or realistic dream might temporarily be confused with wakefulness by virtually anyone from any culture. Occasionally, those of us who collect reported dreams obtain a report prefaced by a statement such as, "I think this was a dream but I'm not sure."

Extraordinary as an example of confusing the dream with wakefulness is the case reported by Raymond De Becker in his book, *The Understanding of Dreams*. An office clerk in Constantine, Algeria, under great emotional stress, surrendered himself to the police as the murderer of his wife and children. Immediate investigation proved that his crime was no more than a dream, but one so vivid that he could hardly be convinced that he had not done what the content of his dream had revealed to him.

Roger Caillois, a French sociologist interested in dreams, believes that most preliterates probably distinguish the dream from wakefulness as experiences on two different, but related, planes. What they, in effect, seem to do is to distinguish between states or types of experience perceived as relevant to one another along some dimension of reality defined by culture.

The dream state is significant because in some meaningful way it relates to the waking state. It is probably safe to say that whenever any human group attributes significance to the dream, the significance of the dream is always interpreted in terms of some kind of meaningful connection between the dream and wakefulness.

Man's occasional perplexity in sorting out dreamed and wakeful experiences and in attributing dominant significance to one over the other is beautifully expressed in the quandary posed by Chuang-tzu, a Chinese philosopher of the third century B.C.

One night I dreamed I was a butterfly, fluttering hither and thither, content with my lot. Suddenly I awoke and again was Chuang-tzu. In reality, who am I? A butterfly dreaming that I am Chuang-tzu or Chuang-tzu dreaming that I am a butterfly?

There are certainly differences among cultural groups in attributing significance to dreams. Broadly speaking, such differences concern the relative importance people attribute to the dream as opposed to wakefulness: in reality, is the importance of dream experience greater than, equal to, or less than that of waking experience? Differences can also concern linkages between the dream and wakefulness: does the dream control waking experience, or does waking experience determine the nature of the dream, or might there be a mutuality between the two states such that each influences the other?

The Mojave, an Indian culture of the American Colorado River Basin, concede to the dream a reality greater than that of wakefulness. The dream is a continuing revelation of the processes of creation granted by the gods to the Mojave. Culture as a meaningful way of life is validated only in the dream. By interpretation at least, the dream controls waking life experience for the Mojave.

For Philippine Negritos, the dream constitutes an equal partner with wakefulness in dealing with reality. Wakefulness and the dream exist on different planes but there is a continuity between them. The reality of the one can influence the reality of the other. A person experiencing an illness or evil dispositions can take them with him from wakefulness into his dreams, hopefully to acquire something from his dreams which he can bring back with him to better serve his needs or the needs of his group in wakefulness. Similarly, a ritual or sacrifice in wakefulness can be taken into the dream to placate the spirits and giants who dwell there.

The significance of the dream in our own culture is that it is regarded as less real than wakefulness. A dominant idea in our culture is that the dream at best constitutes a distortion of reality. When we concede meaning to the dream at all, we see this meaning as a pale or warped reflection of events in our waking lives. For us, waking life dominates the dream, and few of us see the dream as a guide to living more successful waking lives.

Insofar as we can generalize about the significance of the dream in other cultures, it seems that the following points can safely be made. Preliterate people are no more prone to confuse the dream with wakefulness than are people in literate, or more technologically advanced cultures. In any culture the dream is perceived as significant if it is interpreted as meaningful experience. Dream meaning and the value of dream experience are perceived to be in some kind of relationship with reality as defined by culture. The more meaningful dream experience appears to be, and the more clearly it appears to be related to wakeful life, the greater the significance of the dream for any cultural group.

Human Evolution and the Dream

There is probably nothing in man's experience as a species that has failed to contribute to his biological and cultural evolutionary development. The fact that so many different peoples attribute significance to dream experience is evidence of the importance of the dream in cultural evolution.

Whether or not one agrees with the philosopher Nietzsche that the dream and its messages can carry us back to earlier and simpler conditions of human culture (while it also provides us the means for understanding such conditions), the apparent importance of the dream to man in his simpler cultural adaptations is not easily dismissed. Although preliterate cultures do not attribute the same degree of significance to the dream, all generally attribute some significance to it. In such cultures the dream is often recognized as an essential medium through which man can communicate with the cosmos, however defined, can obtain positive sanctions for customary or innovative behaviors, can identify those in the group possessed of extraordinary powers, or can promote greater group and self understanding.

To man in his preliterate cultural conditions, dream experience gives a more extensive world to rely upon than is provided by his waking-life experience. It provides him with a larger margin of cultural creativity than he would have if he were confined to the realities of the world of wakefulness. The cultural uses of dreams in preliterate cultures create for man, according to A. I. Hallowell, a psychological anthropologist, a greater-than-human society which enables him to use greater leverage in dealing with group and individual needs in the continuing processes of cultural adaptation.

The anthropologist Roy D'Andrade, in a study of ethnographic accounts from 63 societies, found great significance ascribed to dreams in the societies wherein sons were expected to move at marriage from their parents' homes and from the local group to which they had become attached as children. The farther away a son had to move at marriage, the greater was the probability that the society would attribute significance to dreams, particularly dreams in which the dreamer sought help from supernatural beings.

D'Andrade also found that dreams were more likely to be considered significant in societies wherein gaining livelihood is more conspicuously an individual rather than a group responsibility. Societies in which there is high individual responsibility are those with hunting, fishing, and animal-husbandry technologies and with an absence of agriculture. Societies in which group responsibility is greater than individual responsibility are societies which have agricultural technologies combined with animal husbandry.

D'Andrade assumes that moving away from one's natal home at marriage and being chiefly responsible for the sustenance of others are anxiety-provoking life experiences. The anxieties thus generated, he believes, are relieved through the person's recourse to the world of dreams. He reasons that it is not accidental that societies which generate these anxieties tend also to be societies which attribute great significance to the dream.

Robert Textor, in a subsequent cross-cultural study, found in general that technologically and socially simpler societies tend to make greater use of the dream than do societies having greater technological and social development. Textor's work both extends and supports D'Andrade's findings. Together, the two studies suggest functional relationships between cultural adaptation and cultural dream use. These functional relationships, however, appear to be complex.

Some Cultural Differences

Some of the Indians from the Colorado River Basin attribute great significance to the dream. The Mojave look to the dream for validation of cultural change. The Yuma believe that the dream reveals whatever has happened or will happen in human experience. In both cultures, dreams constitute an important mechanism, if not the most important, for legitimizing religious belief and practice, interpreting tradition, creating new expressions in song and dance, confirming shamanistic power and curing ability, and validating authority in individuals.

Anyone, in Mojave or Yuma culture, can have a dream to which he or others might attribute special significance. It is common in both cultures for people to have stereotypic dreams relating to the myths of the culture; such dreams always imply significance. While anyone can have a meaningful dream, the more powerful and culturally innovative dreams are expected to originate with dreaming specialists who serve as practitioners in religion or in curing. Not all dreams are valued in a positive way. Dreams of ancestral spirits are particularly frightening. Both these cultures distinguish between ordinary and important dreams. For the Yuma, a dream vision in which the dreamer visits in the realm of the spirits is a much more significant experience than is the ordinary dream, the content of which seems more closely related to the ordinary events of life.

In most cultures that attribute significance to the dream, distinctions are drawn between dreams of greater and those of lesser significance. Distinctions may be made on the basis of the manifest content of the dream, the status of the person who has the dream, or some situation surrounding the occurrence of a dream. For the Mojave and the Yuma any one of these things might be an important factor in determining the significance of a dream.

Dreams were also greatly significant for the people of another American Indian culture, the Iroquois, who occupied territory now chiefly in northeastern United States. A. F. C. Wallace, who has done historical research on the importance of the dream in this society, maintains that the Iroquois had an involved theory of dreams which in certain respects resembles Freud's psychoanalytic dream theory. They believed, for example, that dreams are the products of deep-seated needs or "wishes" in the dreamer. In other words, the dream is seen to have a basic psychological component reflective of the dreamer's deepest motivations. The needs of the dreamer are legitimate needs which seek to find expression in daily life as well as in the dream.

Most dream interpretation among the Iroquois was done by someone other than the dreamer. It was often up to a dreamer's relatives or friends to see that the message of the dream was acted out in suitable form to relieve the dreamer of the tensions or dangers implied in the dream. Hostile or sexual dream fantasy could be acted out in either a direct or symbolic way, so long as the acting-out produced a degree of satisfaction in the dreamer which contributed either to his psychological health or to improved social relations between himself and others.

The Iroquois also had special dreams that they interpreted as messages for the group. Most such dreams were believed to originate with mythological beings or cultural heroes who were protecting the interests of their people. Even a very ordinary person could have such a dream, although normally this kind seemed to have come more often to warriors or chiefs. The individual who revealed a dream of cultural importance, or one that seemed to insure the protection or survival of the dreamer's group, often found himself the recipient of honor and respect. The dreamer, however, was rarely elevated to any special and permanent position of prestige. With time, the significance of his dream contribution was forgotten in the face of subsequent contributions made by other dreamers.

For another example of a culture which attributes high significance to the dream, let us examine the dream theory of the Mae Enga of New Guinea. For the Mae Enga the dream is not inside the individual but rather the individual finds himself inside the dream. This concept of the dream is not unlike that which Piaget finds common in young children. While the Mae Enga in their psychological understanding of the dream may appear to be somewhat childlike, their cultural use of the dream appears to be quite sophisticated.

As with many other cultural groups, the Mae Enga do not attribute equal significance to all dreams. One reason, according to the anthropologist M. J. Meggitt, who studied these people, is that the content of some dreams appears too far removed in meaning from what the dreamer can accept as truth. The Mae Enga do not hesitate to perform what seem to them necessary alterations on dreamed events in order to bring them more in line with the reality of wakefulness or the needs and desires of dreamers.

Whether a dream is significant or not to the Mae Enga depends also in part on the manifest content of the dream. Significant dreams include certain animals, plants, and inanimate things whose presence in a dream is to be taken as evidence of a good or bad omen.

Of greater importance to the significance of the dream is the status of the dreamer. In a local grouping of approximately 350 persons, perhaps no more than five to ten people at one time will have the special status that will make their dreams significant to the group as a whole. These will include the most respected man in the community, usually called "big man." The "big man's" wife or some other mature female who possesses an unusually forceful personality will also fit into the status hierarchy. Other elderly males who serve as diviners, and widowed females, who serve as mediums, also have high status. Occasionally persons, otherwise nondescript except for the fact that they appear to dream significant dreams, will fit into the status hierarchy of significant dreamers. The dreams of young men are also likely to be regarded as significant, particularly during the time of their ritual seclusion as bachelors. The significance of the dreams of these young men disappears with marriage. The dreams of young women and children of both sexes are rarely regarded as significant.

The significance of Mae Enga dreams is essentially social. Dreams help determine the course of many social decisions. Dreams, generally, define and exemplify the values of the culture. A person remiss in certain obligations to others may be visited by ghosts or ancestors who point out the paths to be followed in correct social behavior. Interpretations of dreams often are in the nature of decisions made by or for the dreamer in line with the values of his society.

Although there are some symbols which mark certain dreams as significant, many dreams are regarded by the Mae Enga as uninterpretable for the average dreamer. If a dream is felt to be significant but not easily interpreted, it will be referred to a dream expert or "man of knowledge" for interpretation. Experts are those whose own dreams are likely to be considered significant. These experts look well beyond the manifest content of the dreams presented to them. In the Freudian idiom, they appear to look for the latent or disguised meaning of the dream. In trying to determine the meaning or significance of a given dream, dream experts appear to look more toward the social situation of the dreamer than they do toward the manifest content of his dream. Dream experts obviously function more as arbiters of the social system than they do as exclusive interpreters of the Mae Enga dream world.

Many North American Indian tribes other than those mentioned attached great significance to dreams. Of special significance to Indians over a wide geographical area were guardian-spirit dreams. Guardian-spirit dreams of one kind or another have been described for many of the different cultural groups distributed over the Eastern Woodlands, the Plains, even the Northwest Coast.

Among the Winnebago, an Eastern Woodland tribe, preadolescent children of both sexes would seek the attentions of a guardian spirit whom they believed would help them in future life crises. The way to get the attention of a spirit was to fast. Some individuals approached the fast with great fervor and serious intent. Others apparently did not, according to Paul Radin, a student of Winnebago culture.

If a child was successful in his quest, he would obtain a message or a dream vision from the guardian spirit who was to be his guide in adult life. If a guardian spirit failed to appear to a child in his dreams, the fault was assumed to rest with the insincerity and playfulness of the child. He or she was admonished by his elders to try again, but with greater sincerity. Many appeals, with fasting, could be made to obtain the favored appearance of a guardian spirit.

Among the Menomini, also a Woodland culture, greater emphasis was placed on the necessary sincerity of the fasters, and greater gravity was attached to the nature of the dream vision. Young men and women about fifteen years of age were to engage in a strict fast and pray from eight to ten days for a dream signifying good life prospects for the dreamer.

Menomini youths were urged to keep their minds on the higher things of life and on things above the earth, where the good powers dwell. To dream eventually of something from on high was a good omen, denoting greatness, power, happiness, and a long life for the dreamer. To dream of something under the skies was a waste of time. To dream of something under the earth was a portent of an evil to befall the dreamer.

Parents of Menomini adolescents, seeing that the dreams of their children might not be going well, would command them to break their fasts and try again at some more auspicious time, or when the youth was better disposed to dream of higher things. In any case the dream quest was to be terminated after the third vision. The nature of the dream then had to be accepted, even if it denoted evil.

Plains Indian cultures stressed even more the significance of the guardian-spirit dream. Ruth Benedict and George Devereux, among other anthropologists who have studied Plains Indian cultures, have indicated the distinctive characteristics of the guardian-spirit quest in Plains cultures. Among the more important distinctions was the greater emphasis which Plains cultures placed on the individual's responsibilities to obtain favorable dream visions. The infliction of self-torture, in addition to fasting, to insure obtaining a desirable dream vision was an important characteristic of most of the Plains cultures. An interesting cultural exception in this regard was that of the Omaha, who used neither fasting nor self-torture in the dream quest.

According to Erik Erikson, a noted psychoanalyst and also a student of culture, the Dakota used dreams to guide the strong in following basic cultural values and ideals. They also used dreams to set limits on deviations among the weak. As did youths from other Plains Indian groups, the Dakota youth would seek dreams to guide him in the proper course for his adult life. Physically separating himself from others in his encampment, lightly clad and without food, the youth wandered into the prairie. There, after declaring his great unworthiness, he would beseech his guardian spirit for guidance. After deliberately exposing himself to heat, hunger, thirst, and the possible attack of predators, he would patiently await a message from the spirit. The dream message from the supernatural guardian was usually expected on the fourth day of his ordeal. If the dream was tardy, self-torture and mutilation would be used to persuade the guardian spirit of the good intent of the supplicant. To cut off a finger joint was not considered too great a sacrifice to obtain the prompt attention of one's spiritual guardian.

Despite the sufferings undergone to obtain a dream vision, the message of the Dakota youth's dreams was usually interpreted to indicate that he should do extraordinarily well the ordinary things of life. Infrequently, dreams were taken to indicate possibilities in cultural innovation, usually concerned with the inventions of new prayers, songs, dances, or healing techniques. But dreams also might mark a Dakota youth as a tribal functionary, a curer, or a religious practitioner, or foretell that he would become a great chief.

Dreams could also confirm deviancy, but only in certain restricted ways permitted by the culture. One notable type of deviancy sanctioned by many Plains cultures permitted young males, if they lacked the aggressive dispositions to become warriors and hunters, to take on a passive role resembling that of females in their societies.

Dreams and visions among the Plains Indians were not always as personal, or as personally relevant to the dreamer, as would seem to be the case with guardian-spirit dreams. According to Robert Lowie, an anthropologist who worked among the Crow Indians, a dream that put the dreamer in contact with the spirit world was an extraordinary dream, or dream vision. Such dreams always had religious or ceremonial significance and were relevant to one or another aspect of the social life of the people.

So important were such dream visions, according to Lowie, that they could be bought and sold to insure their distribution among people who never experienced them. An individual who sought access to a certain supernatural power would also buy the vision which accompanied the power.

The Crow did not distinguish linguistically between dreams and dream visions. Both experiences were called by the same term. But the significance of a dream vision over an ordinary dream was momentous. Dream visions were remembered in great detail while ordinary dreams were forgotten almost as soon as they transpired. Lowie was able readily to obtain elaborate texts of dream visions, but despite great effort was unable to collect any detailed reports of ordinary dreams.

Guardian-spirit dreams are also found in other parts of the world. Dreams of secret helpers are one such example, from the Sea Dyaks of Borneo. Unlike the Dakota, for example, men among the Sea Dyaks do not all desire protection from a secret helper. A young man who does desire such a spirit guardian will attend to his quest in much the same fashion as does the Plains Indian youth. The young Dyak will deliberately detach himself from his group, fast in seclusion, and await the response of his guardian spirit in dreams.

The Dyak secret helper is an ancestor of the supplicant. He will appear to his protégé first in human form. In later appearances he will take the form of an animal. Because of the dreamed appearance of the secret helper in animal form, living animals of the same kind fall under the special respect of the dreamer. The dreamer will neither kill nor eat the flesh of the animal who represents his guardian. Secret helpers tend to become centers of family cults. A man who has been particularly dutiful and respectful to a secret helper expects to find that help extended to his children and grandchildren, who continue to honor the secret helper as a special protector of the family.

Even when cultures attribute different significance to dreams, dreams may serve a similar function in relieving psychological stress in dreamers.

The anthropologist Bronislaw Malinowski tells us that the Trobriand Islanders of Melanesia show almost no interest in ordinary dreams. That is, they attach little significance to them. They have no explanation for ordinary dreaming and no system for decoding the symbols of ordinary dreams. Malinowski calls ordinary dreams "free dreams." Contrasted with "free dreams" are "official dreams," which can be controlled by magic and sorcery. Official dreams are induced, and their manifest content relates to things of special interest to people: trading expeditions, fishing, gardening, and making love. A person's dreams are largely controlled by forces outside himself.

The Tikopians, a Polynesian people, differ in that they attribute great significance to their dreams, according to Raymond Firth, an anthropologist who studied them. They do not make the same distinctions among their dreams as do the Trobriand Islanders. For the Tikopians, the dream is an adventure of the spirit. Dream experience, in fact, is taken as evidence of the spirit world to which everyone has access. The dream is a creation of the spirit world, being the outcome of what is enacted there.

It is possible to make a comparison of the significance of incest dreams between the two cultures. A Trobriand Islander believes in the actuality of the dreamed incest and it provokes shame within him. The Tikopian believes, on the other hand, that he has been seduced by an evil spirit from the dream world in the guise of a close relative. Such a dream produces for the Tikopian not shame but fear. He has not committed incest but has had intercourse with an evil spirit. The act from his dream will bring on misfortune, debilitation, or illness.

Dreams produced by magic, in the belief system of the Trobriand Islanders, create in dreamers desires not necessarily their own. Such wishes are imposed on the dreamers, although the dreamer does in fact participate in his own dream experience. Tikopians customarily blame spirits for forcing or duping dreamers to engage in morally despicable behavior. When the Trobriand Islander blames the magic of someone else for his dreamed act, or when the Tikopian blames an evil spirit for his, the functional outcome is somewhat the same. Both cultures make use of a "pass the buck" explanation for dreams whose content runs contrary to the moral standards of wakefulness.

The Significance of the Dream in History

Written references to dreams make their appearance almost as early in human history as does writing itself. This antiquity, and the fact that references to the dream appear in many kinds of literature, attest to the significance man has attributed to the dream over history.

Some of the earliest dream literature is found in a "dream book" attributed to the Egyptian Pharaoh Merikare, about 2070 B.C. The text indicates that dreams were thought to be intuitive forays into the future. Fragments of later Egyptian texts on dreams survive from about 1800 B.C. Some of the very early Egyptian papyri also include references to dreams. Bestiality and incest appear to have been either common themes in Egyptian dreams, or themes which interpreters regarded as being particularly significant. Dreams appear to have been simply interpreted as either good or bad omens without giving the dreamer any detail about what he could expect as the result of having had a certain dream. The interpretation of some dream material appears to be opposite to what one would expect from the manifest content of the dream. For example, a theme denoting happiness might be interpreted as a bad omen.

The most ancient Assyrian dream literature deals extensively with themes of eating and drinking. The ancient Assyrians seem to have been preoccupied with the eating of human flesh in their dreams, especially the body parts of the dreamer's self or his close relatives. By 600 B.C. the Assyrians believed that bad dreams were caused by afflictions and that they could be relieved if a dream could be interpreted well enough to reveal the source of the affliction.

The first specific interpretations for dream symbols, linking a symbol to wakeful experience or a future event, seems to have arisen in India. Ancient Hinduism was much concerned with the significance of the dream from both divine and human perspectives. Hindu theology suggests that the world is a dream of Brahma. In the *Atharva Veda*, the writers attempt to make possible the interpretation of dream images with reference to the temperament of the dreamer and astrological signs pertinent to his life situation.

The dream was significant also to the ancient Chinese. Dreams were felt to be reflections of some important aspect of human experience. Inasmuch as human experience was perceived to be unitary, the dream was interpreted to be an integral part of total human experience. The Chinese employed elaborate systems of interpretation to get at the meaning of dreams. Astrological and geometric computations entered into dream interpretation in China in the fourth century B.C. The *I Ching* (an oracular *Book of Changes*) is composed of hexagrams based on symbolic images which were applied to dream imagery as well as to other mysterious patterns in human experience. Chinese dream interpretation seems never to have been purely a matter of symbolic or mechanical interpretation despite the intricate formulas developed by dream interpreters. Proper dream interpretation depended greatly on the context of the dream with reference to important events in the dreamer's life. To what extent the social situation of the dreamer or his psychological state was perceived to be important in his total life context is not clearly discernible in the Chinese literature. Factors deemed important in assessing the dream meaning were: the year, season, and day of the dream, sometimes including the part of the night in which the dream occurred; astrological factors; and the respective situations of the great energy forces of Yin and Yang.

The significance of the dream for the Chinese Taoists was in the attainment of greater self-knowledge. Dreams were classified according to cause. The cause of a dream was important because it revealed physical and mental changes taking place in the dreamer, changes which if understood permitted the dreamer better to cope with his personal problems through self knowledge.

In the classical civilizations of the West, the meaning of dreams seems to have fallen into four broad classifications: divinatory dreams revealing the hidden future, oracular dreams revealing the hidden present, incubation dreams induced for curing, and natural dreams representing ordinary biological and psychological needs.

Hippocrates, the father of Western medicine, and later Aristotle, placed somewhat greater emphasis on the importance of natural dreams than did most of their contemporaries or those who came after them. They attributed diagnostic significance to natural dreams.

Out of the rich patrimony that modern Western culture inherited from the Greeks, probably the most important ideas concerning the significance of the dream came to us from Artemidorus of Daldis, who lived in the second century A.D. In his *Oneirocritica,* Artemidorus takes a surprisingly modern look at the significance of dreams. He tried to dispel the notion that there are absolute rules of dream interpretation. He insisted that to understand a dream one must know much concerning the dreamer himself, his sex, age, origins, status, occupations, and other important social indices.

Many of the dream books produced in Europe after the Renaissance are at least partly traceable to the work of Artemidorus. Unfortunately, in the main they are slavish and mechanical derivations of his work, devoid of the flexible and sophisticated approach to dream understanding that Artemidorus tried to develop. Most such dream books were dictionaries of dream symbols to which meanings were assigned on the basis of folklore or the work of earlier authorities, sometimes of ancient origin.

The Romans, too, attributed significance to the dream, but apparently added little by way of innovative thinking to what they had borrowed from the Greeks and from other great civilizations of the ancient world. It seems that dreams were most important to the Romans for divinatory and oracular purposes. Roman writers often distinguished between true and false dreams. The Roman Virgil, apparently following the Greek Homer, maintains in the *Aeneid* that true dreams come through the Gate of Horn and visit the dreamer after midnight, while false dreams come through the Gate of Ivory and visit the dreamer before midnight. False dreams seem to have been governed more by physiological functions, excessive tiredness, or digestive disturbances. True dreams seem to have been governed more by supernatural factors, messages or assistance from the gods. The distinction between true and false dreams appears related to ideas that were current among peoples in other civilizations at that time.

The idea of the divinatory significance of dreams did not go unchallenged in the Roman world. Cicero, who was particularly skeptical of the idea, questioned its rationality. The certainty of the divinatory function of the dream as a message from the gods to man was not easily settled even by dream interpreters. This being the case, Cicero questioned why the gods should communicate themselves to men in such an unreliable manner.

Dreams had dual significance in Judaism. Dreams, as messages from God or visitations from angels, appear as significant events in the Pentateuch. The possibly good or evil significance of dreams in Judaism is reflected in the Babylonian Talmud, written between the sixth and second centuries B.C. It is replete with references to dreams, with rules both for interpreting and avoiding them.

There seems to have been great popular interest in dreams among the ancient Jews, which probably reflected some common cultural traits among peoples in the pre-Christian Near East regarding the significance of dreams. Interpreting dreams as messages from multiple divine and demonic sources appears to have been important in attributing significance to dreams in Near Eastern civilizations. The polytheistic implications of attributing significance to dreams in that area of the world at that time possibly stood as a threat to the delicately balanced monotheistic beliefs which the Jews struggled so hard to preserve. As one result of this struggle, the popular interest in dreams was countered among the Jews with an official religious position which played down the significance of dreams.

The dualistic attitude toward dreams and the minimization of their significance carried over historically from Judaism both to Islam and to Christianity. Probably because of the influence of other Near Eastern civilizations on Islam, dreams have retained a higher level of significance in Islamic cultures than they have in Christian cultures. Mohammed believed the dream to be a conversation between man and Allah. But while any of the faithful might have a significant dream, interpretation is cautiously left only to the most devout.

The dual significance of the dream, with either divine or diabolic origin, and the ambiguity which surrounded it, eventually contributed to its greater decline in Christianity. While some of the early Christian Fathers regarded the dream as potentially important for receiving divine illumination, the dreamer nevertheless was usually cautioned against the potential dangers of his dream. St. Cyprian, St. Cyril, and Tertullian had positive regard for the dream. St. Augustine and St. Ambrose composed prayers to be spared from dreaming. After the early medieval period the dream came more and more into disrepute in official church teaching. Medieval literature sometimes referred to the dream as "nocturnal terror."

As in Judaism, dreams maintained some popular appeal in Christianity even though officially opposed by churchmen. During the Middle Ages and almost in the pattern of the pagan past, even though the practice had been officially condemned by the Church, the incubation of dreams occurred in important Christian churches such as the Basilica of St. Martin of Tours in France and the Augustinian Monastery in Donegal, Ireland. In the incubation of dreams, a supplicant sought through prayer and fasting in a holy setting to receive dreams through which he might be relieved of physical or spiritual illness.

St. Thomas Aquinas, held to be one of the greatest thinkers in Catholicism, held some rather interesting views on dreams. He believed in the possible divination of dreams. But dreams, even if they revealed truth, were sinful because divination always implicates the devil. He also believed that premonitions in dreams might be cause rather than foreteller of future events. The dream might serve as an inspiration, or at least a motor force propelling the dreamer toward achieving a goal in wakefulness.

The assumed divinatory nature of dreams linked them in time with witchcraft. The nature of dreams, with the frequent themes of sexuality and aggression commonly found in manifest content, were attributed to the devil. In the fifteenth and sixteenth centuries dreams sometimes stood as the only damning evidence to be brought against a witch. The *Malleus Maleficarum*, used as a handbook of the inquisition, advised the burning at the stake of dreamers who had come into league with Satan. Some of the ointments and medications of witches (belladonna, henbane, the seeds from poppies and morning glories) may indeed have induced dreams or hallucinations.

The effects of the Reformation on dream thought were not immediately apparent. Works by Benedict Pererius (for Catholics) and Gaspar Pencer (for Protestants) in the late 1500s do not widely diverge in what they have to say about dreams. Theological differences had not spread to opinions on the religious significance of the dream.

Martin Luther believed that self-knowledge could be obtained in dreams. One could study his dreams to find his sins and repent of them. Dream study should lead to an understanding of the artifices of the devil, of which the good Christian should not be ignorant. Yet Luther saw danger in dreams and prayed that God would not speak to him in this way. John Calvin believed that God sometimes spoke to the devout in dreams but always in an allegorical or obscure way, leaving the person in a quandary. John Calvin also seemed not to have a high regard for dreams.

In a more recent time the establishment of the Church of Latter Day Saints was attributed to dream revelations made to Joseph Smith. In 1820, Smith dreamed of the establishment of the church at the bidding of God the Father and the Son. In 1823, Smith dreamed of the Angel Moroni, who revealed to him the existence of the Book of Mormon.

The individual Christian interested in the religious significance of dreams has continuously faced the problem of having to distinguish the supernatural from the natural dream, and then, in the supernatural dream, of having to discern what is from God as opposed to what might be from the devil. The individual Christian in recent centuries has been influenced more by secular than by religious thought concerning dreams. Books on the religious signif- icance of dreams for contemporary Christians have been written by Morton Kelsey (*Dreams: The Dark Speech of the Spirit*), and John Sanford (*Dreams: God's Forgotten Language*). It is really not yet clear whether the appearance of such books is indicative of a substantial and growing interest in the dream by religious thinkers.

The Significance of the Dream for Science

René Descartes, seventeenth-century mathematician and philosopher, is credited with exerting a profound influence on the development of contem- porary Western thought. Cartesian thought influenced deeply the tendencies of Western man to dichotomize phenomena falling within his range of experience, because Descartes felt that not all experiences were equally trustworthy in revealing reality to man. Ultimately, empirical truth is to be tested by the yardstick of rationality. The very nature of dream experience tended to put the dream more firmly into the realm of irrational experience in emerging naturalistic and scientific thought. Ironically, Descartes's ideas emerged from a set of his personal dream experiences—ideas which served to depress the significance of the dream in modern scientific thought even more than did the Judaic-Christian traditions.

Outright skepticism or general noninterest seems to have been the stance of the Western man toward the dream during the eighteenth century. But, with a growing impetus to freer inquiry in all things, interest in the dream revived in nineteenth-century Europe. A great gulf separated those who became inter- ested in dreams. Romantics, mostly poets and literary figures, fervently sought to keep the dream on the purely expressive and irrational plane. Naturalists, including scientists and philosophers, enthusiastically sought to bring the dream to the natural plane of inquiry.

For the most part rationalist thinkers took a simplified view of the dream, attributing it basically to physiological functions such as indigestion, muscle cramps, temperature changes, and conditions relating to the general comfort or discomfort of the body in sleep. Psychologists and physiologists of the 1800s studied dream content in relation to bodily functions in themselves or others.

In France, Alfred Maury was one of the more illustrious of these. His thesis was that dreams are the manifestations of memories being unlocked in the dreamer as a result of external stimuli experienced in sleep. On one occasion, Maury dreamed that he was tried before a tribunal in the French Revolution. Found guilty, he was sentenced to the guillotine. As the blade of the dream guillotine dropped, Maury awoke to find that a loose head board from the bed had fallen on his neck. He interpreted the accident to be the simple stimulus which unlocked his complex dream experience. He is one of those responsible for the widespread belief that even complex dreams occur within a split second of time, a belief which more recent laboratory research seems not to support. Karl Scherner, a German, was convinced that careful analyses of dreams would eventually lead to a clear understanding of their origins in the experiences of the dreamer. He also recognized and placed emphasis upon the symbolic character of dream language. Scherner appears to have had a great influence on Freud. Havelock Ellis, the famous English psychologist, tried to understand why emotions appear to be so greatly intensified in dreams. He found that even the simplest of external stimuli applied in sleep often evoked bizarre and dramatic dream memories. He called attention to the fact that vividly dramatic content seems to occur in order to express the intensification of the affective state in dreaming. Recent findings pinpointing intense activity in the brainstem in REM sleep suggest physiological answers to some of Ellis's questions.

Without doubt the work of Sigmund Freud was the most important effort within Western science to establish the significance of the dream for modern man. Freud's talents, not only for analyzing dream material but for synthesizing prevailing ideas, enabled him to create a theory that centralized the dream in the mental and emotional life of man. Freud shifted emphasis in thought on the dream from the physiological and external to the psychological and internal range of experience.

In the nineteenth century, scientific interest in the dream came more and more to fall under the aegis of psychology, which along with the several behavioral and social disciplines was beginning to take its own place as a distinct science. Within psychology, however, interest in the dream was mostly limited to speculations or experiments on the effects of sleep and presleep stimuli on resulting dreams. Although this work was never discontinued, it was overshadowed by clinical interest in the dream after Freud's momentous statement on the psychoanalytic significance of the dream.

The failure of laboratory dream research to gain momentum even by 1953, the same year in which Aserinsky and Kleitman published their exciting research on the rapid movement of the eyes in dreaming, caused the psychologist Glenn Ramsey to report disparagingly on the paltry and deficient state of dream research. The dream had become, rather than a matter of focal interest in general psychology, a subject of parochial interest largely limited to certain segments of the broader field. Defensively, various theoretical camps within psychology created barriers to a continuing generalized dialogue on dreams. Paradoxically, conceptualizations on the dream within the segments of psychology often had a greater impact on people in disciplines outside psychology than they did on people in other psychologically oriented disciplines. For example, the impact of Freudian dream thought on anthropology was immeasurably greater than it was on behaviorist, social, or gestalt psychology.

Because the anthropologist needs to attend to those things which have meaning for the people he studies, and because many of the peoples encountered by anthropologists have attributed significance to their dreams, there has been a traditional but somewhat variable stance over time toward the significance of the dream in anthropology. Beginning with Sir Edward Tylor, who developed a theory that dreams probably constituted one of the most important factors in the evolution of human religion, anthropologists from about 1870 to the turn of the century took great ethnographic and historical interest in the dreams of the people they studied. From the early 1900s to about the middle 1930s, Freudian theory had a great impact on anthropologists seeking answers to the psychological dispositions of people in different cultures. One dominant approach was the attempt to understand articulations between the dynamics of culture and the development of personality. Freudian applications were not always practical for the anthropologist, however, and interest in dreams declined in anthropology. More recently it has experienced a revival. Non-Freudian methods of dream collection and analysis focusing on manifest content, championed by Dorothy Eggan and others, have pointed to new promise for dream study in anthropology, particularly in cross-cultural perspective.

The dream is coming to the attention of people in other disciplines as well. The exciting laboratory research of the 1950s functioned as a catalyst to reestablish the importance of experimental studies to generate interdisciplinary research in the dream, and to recharge a flagging concern with the development of dream theory. By 1962, the impetus for interdisciplinary approaches to dream study had grown to the point where an international conference on the social significance of the dream was held in France. The colloquium attracted scholars internationally, not only from the biological, psychological, and social sciences, but also from the cultural, historical, and humanistic disciplines. Western culture, at last, may be finding significance in the dream.

4

PHYSIOLOGICAL AND PSYCHOLOGICAL DREAM FUNCTIONS

The most profitable aspect of dream study since the 1960s has been the efforts to understand the dream in its relationship to sleep. Measurements of shifts in physiological activity have become our most reliable means for determining stages of sleep. REM sleep, with dreaming, is characterized by an intensification of certain physiological functions and a deceleration of others. For example, the heart rate is speeded, pulse and respiration become erratic, and as was previously mentioned the eyes move vigorously. The brain stem chiefly but also other parts of the brain become intensely active with a noticeable rise in temperature. Nevertheless, the body as a whole and particularly the large skeletal muscles are deeply relaxed during this time of great inner turbulence.

The close correspondence between experiencing a dream and experiencing certain rather unique and intense physiological activities suggests a functional connection between the dream and these activities. What these connections may be are still not well understood. It was tempting for a while to think that the psychological processes of dreaming might have some dominant role to play in the physiological processes of REM sleep. In other words, some evidence from sleep and dream studies in the laboratory had suggested that there might be a need for man to dream, a need so basic that it calls into play certain physiological processes as a concomitant to the dream state. Few researchers entertain these theories at present because it seems that the overwhelming evidence from the laboratory emphasizes the priority of physiological events over psychological events in REM sleep.

Disordered Sleep and Dreaming

Just as there are malfunctions in other parts of nature, there are malfunctions attending the cycles of sleep and dreaming. It is to be hoped that in a study of these, the victims of the malfunctions will be helped and also that we will gain a deeper knowledge of what the sleep and dream cycles are and of how they contribute to human well being.

Narcolepsy is one malfunction of the sleep and dream cycles. Often it is described as a condition of inappropriate sleep because narcoleptics have little or no control over falling asleep at inappropriate times. Symptoms of narcolepsy are difficult to distinguish from indications of ordinary sleepiness. Attacks may last for only a few seconds so that persons with the narcoleptic, or the victim himself, may not realize that one has occurred. Other attacks may be more prolonged and more severe in their consequences, so that the narcoleptic may be a danger to himself or others. An attack while the narcoleptic is driving, for instance, may precipitate a serious accident. Severe attacks may put the victim into a state of apparent paralysis, at which time he is also likely to experience hallucinations. The seizures are called cataplexy. About 60% of narcoleptics experience cataplexy. After such an attack the victim remains relatively immobilized for a short period of time, finding it difficult to relate to his environment.

Sometimes even the experiences of mild emotions—pleasant, such as unexpectedly meeting an old friend; or unpleasant, such as having to discipline one's child—can induce attacks of narcolepsy. Some narcoleptics are particularly susceptible to rhythmic motions such as dancing which might precipitate a seizure.

Allan Rechtschaffen and his associates, at the sleep and dream laboratories of the University of Chicago, have confirmed that the various symptoms of narcolepsy are representative of the various stages of sleep. The cataplexy of the narcoleptic, as measured by the electroencephalograph (EEG), turns out to be REM sleep. Normal persons only gradually attain REM sleep after some 80 to 90 minutes of quiet, or NREM, sleep. Many narcoleptics, however, in a severe attack literally fall into REM sleep, precipitously and without warning. Physical collapse, appearing as temporary paralysis, is caused by the sudden loss of muscle tone in the body, which is what occurs normally to everyone in REM sleep. This loss of muscle tone poses no problem for the average individual because it occurs for him as he lies safely asleep in his bed.

Some narcoleptics, it has been discovered, seem to have less REM sleep at night than do normals. Whether this difference is due to having REM sleep in the form of daytime attacks is not clear. Narcoleptics who use such drugs as the amphetamines to control their attacks in the daytime also suppress REM sleep at night.

Some interesting questions relate to an understanding of the narcoleptic condition. One such question might be phrased this way: "Is there a psychological need on the part of the narcoleptic to go into an immediate state of dream sleep as a result of his daytime experiences?" Some evidence indicates that there may be. If so, an argument could be made that an inordinate or uncontrolled need to dream would be the inducement to spontaneous and severe narcoleptic attacks.

While the hypothesis underlying the question is an interesting one, and one which may still merit some consideration, it appears not to be the most reasonable hypothesis, given our present state of knowledge. The evidence is that while the narcoleptic indeed may have an inordinate and uncontrolled need for REM sleep, this need is the result of metabolic malfunction rather than psychological urgency.

Dream and Sleep Deprivation

Another area of research which has prompted questions relating to the psychological primacy of the dream as an instigator of REM sleep has been that of the so-called dream-deprivation experiments. The question underlying this research was essentially, "Do we sleep in order to dream?"

In the early 1960s, William Dement and Charles Fisher at Mount Sinai Hospital in New York attempted to answer the question of what would happen to a person deprived of the REM sleep in which dreaming appeared to be such an important psychological activity. Volunteers in the dream laboratory were deprived of some of their REM sleep by being awakened after the start of each REM stage. After the awakenings they generally lapsed into NREM sleep. In this procedure 65 percent of REM sleep and dream time was lost, enough loss to produce dramatic effects in the volunteers. Other phases of sleep were not interrupted and the total sleep time was left constant.

Dreamers so deprived attempted to compensate for the loss by lapsing into dream stages more quickly than their normal patterns indicated they should. More importantly, in wakefulness following such deprivation, volunteers usually suffered from anxiety and other forms of psychological distress.

With the end of the deprivation experiments the volunteers were allowed to sleep without interruption. In this recovery period REM sleep with dreaming occurred more frequently and lasted longer than was the case in the normal pattern. It was as though those persons who had suffered REM sleep and dream deprivation were trying to catch up on their sleep—or was it on their dreaming?

Such early results indicative of psychological deterioration were frequently interpreted as the primary consequences of dream deprivation because overall sleep time was left constant. The hypothesis that the dream represents a basic human need which must be met to maintain health and well being was an attractive one. It seemed to some that we may sleep in order to dream and not dream simply in order to sleep as Freud and others have maintained.

An example of one dream-deprivation experiment follows. The effects of 16 nights of dream deprivation were intensively studied for one subject. For control purposes his basic sleep patterns were studied for 12 nights prior to the experimentation. Performance tests such as speed of perception, memory, and tracking ability were administered to him under both control and experimental conditions; so also were projective tests.

The effects of dream deprivation were not clearly apparent until about the sixth night of the experiment. First, there were complaints of apathy and fatigue. By the ninth night, the subject became demonstrably irritable at being awakened. His coordination, attention, and memory declined to levels where it became necessary for him to quit driving his car. Eventually he became so drowsy and his need for REM sleep became so overpowering that he began to lapse into spontaneous naps much as the narcoleptic appears to do. To prevent his taking naps he had to punch a watchman's clock every fifteen minutes. In the final days of the experiment he had to be attended constantly by a personal friend. Over the course of the experiment he became less and less responsive to others. He avoided mental activity when possible and increasingly attempted to escape observation by others. Near the end of the deprivation study, the subject, who under more normal conditions indicated no particular interest in the topic of homosexuality, became more and more interested in that topic.

In his responses to performance and projective tests, the subject revealed what seemed to be severe psychological transformations taking place in his customary behavior. For example, stimuli which had been interpreted by the subject under control conditions as geometric configurations after several nights of dream deprivation were interpreted as grotesque and threatening animated figures.

Man's need for dreaming appeared to be so basic and so protected by natural mechanisms controlling its occurrence that it seemed to be literally impossible to deprive some persons of this experience, even partially, for more than short periods of time.

In one experiment by Dement, endeavoring to deprive them of all REM dream sleep for 16 consecutive nights, subjects were awakened by a sensitive electronic device just before an REM period was due to begin. After 8 nights one subject became virtually immune to any attempt to awaken him. If the experimenters succeeded, he would immediately fall back into REM dream sleep rather than NREM sleep. The procedure of attempted deprivation got to the point at which it became necessary to try to repeat it every few seconds.

So strongly did this subject's need to dream seem to be asserting itself that it became impossible to deprive him of this segment of sleep without depriving him of all sleep.

It seems necessary to make two points here concerning the dream-deprivation experiments. The first concerns ethics. Obviously, experiments with the possibilities of such drastic results should not be lightly undertaken. Yet harsh as some of these experiments seem to have been, necessary safeguards were always employed by the experimenters; they were well aware of their ethical obligations to their subjects and professionally competent to make the necessary judgments relevant to these ethical obligations. Subjects for the dream-deprivation experiments were always carefully screened psychologically to insure their emotional stability. Often they were volunteers who had previously undergone other sleep and dream experiments. Sometimes they were members of the professional and technical staffs of the dream laboratories.

Precautions were always taken in the course of experiments to insure that no one would suffer real or permanent damage. Experiments were terminated at the first sign that they might be physically or psychologically endangering the subject. Subjects were further afforded the necessary safeguards to protect them from adverse effects of dream deprivation in their waking-life activities.

Some element of risk always attaches itself to human efforts to learn more about man and his world. It seems that no undue risks were taken with the lives or welfare of subjects who underwent dream- and sleep-deprivation experiments. On the other hand, we have considerably advanced the knowledge we have of ourselves as a result of these experiments.

The second point is a more technical one, relating to the question of the significance of dream deprivation. What have we learned? The earlier work in this area was often interpreted in terms of dream deprivation rather than in terms of deprivation of REM sleep. It seemed as though we indeed do sleep to dream. Minimal deprivation was accompanied by the attempt on the part of the organism to recoup lost dream time. More severe deprivation was accompanied by manifestations of psychological distress. It seemed as though a psychological need to dream dominated physiological activities in the sleep cycle.

But as research has accumulated since the mid 1960s, it has become more and more apparent that whatever function sleep serves in any of its phases, that function is related to a re-creation of the total human organism more basically than to serving psychological processes primarily. Ian Oswald and his associates at the University of Edinburgh have come up with evidence that REM sleep is essential for the growth and regeneration of the brain. There is a close parallel between brain growth and the need for REM sleep in the developing organism. Brain-cell growth and renewal is very rapid in the earliest period of human life. In later years, brain-cell growth appears to cease entirely and even brain-cell renewal may become severely retarded. REM sleep appears only slightly diminished with normal aging. It is more seriously reduced in aging when physiological deterioration contributes to senility.

No definitive answers have yet been found concerning the full range of functions to be attributed to sleep and dreaming. Our best answers are still at an early theoretical stage of development. At this point it seems most reasonable to assume that the dream, as a psychological experience, is a by-product of physiological events rather than the other way around. But if this eventually proves to be the case, it will not necessarily diminish the significance of the dream. It seems that the dream stands as an important aspect of total human experience which we can ill afford to ignore, at least within a psychological context.

Psychological Theories of Dream Function

Not all theories attach equal importance to the dream in what it does for man in sleep. Some physiologically oriented psychologists see the dream simply as a working off of metabolites (products of metabolism) in the brain, a process that creates internal sensations and imagery of a mentally primitive order. Others see the dream as a process of memory junking, in which mental trivia gathered in wakefulness are disposed of during sleep. This latter process is analogous to the clearing away of accumulated clutter from a computer.

Each of these theories suggests great inefficiency, according to Walter Bonime, a psychiatrist at New York Medical College. Yet dreams in their normal structure and content do not suggest such functional inefficiency on the part of the nervous system. Laboratory studies and clinical observations made on the manifest content of dreams suggest great selectivity and organi-zation of material in the dreaming process. Even if the dream constitutes only a system of memory filing, then that system is indeed elaborate, involving a vast network of subsystems centralized through an intricate and continuously updated cross-index system. Few psychologists are content to see the dream simply as an expression of physiological functions devoid of psychological significance. To discount the psychological significance of the dream is to run the risk of discounting much of the wisdom of the human unconscious.

An important division in human thinking about the dream arose very early in man's recorded history. Before we examine this, we should be aware that the two modes of thought are not necessarily dichotomous approaches to understanding the functions of the dream whether in historical thought or in current theory. Apparently, the two modes of thought have stood side by side in some systems of dream interpretation beginning with that of the ancient Egyptians and continuing up to more recent formulations. But any system of dream thought which accommodates both approaches must emphasize one over the other.

One approach accepts dream symbolism as a mental process revealing the deep realities of man's experience. The other approach interprets dream symbolism as a disguise of the psychological expressions of basic human needs. The first approach sees the dream as the more direct representation of human needs and aspirations. The second approach sees the dream as the less direct representation of the operation of primary forces in human behavior. The implications of each approach call for somewhat different formulations of the understanding of dream function. What these approaches have in common is the basic assumption that the dream does serve important psychological functions. Where they diverge is in postulating what these functions are and how they operate as psychological mechanisms in human behavior. In modern times, the second approach is that of Sigmund Freud and those who subscribe to his theory. The first approach, not so clearly defined as a single approach because of the greater diversity of ideas associated with it, embraces in modern times the various positions of Carl Jung, Alfred Adler, and many contemporary theorists who take what have been labeled "cognitive," "Gestalt," "integrative," and "phenomenological" positions on the dream.

Freud's contributions to theory on the functions of dreams were uniquely stimulating to the mind of Western man. Freud maintained that the dream represents expressions of deep-seated instinctual (that is, biologically based) yearnings, mostly of a sexual nature, largely unsatisfied and repressed in conscious experience. These he called "wishes." Wishes are rarely clearly represented in a dream because they often run counter to the internalized value system of the dreamer and would, if manifestly expressed, disrupt the flow of sleep.

According to Freud, the dream has two purposes: to represent or fulfill wishes and to guard sleep. To achieve these purposes, dream work functions to achieve, by symbolism, a compromise between the assertion and disguise of wishes. The true, the more important, and the latent meaning of the dream is the wish; the disguised, less important, and manifest expression of the dream is the symbol.

The manifest content is a product of dream work and is constructed by the organism during sleep in its attempt to derive fulfillment for its wishes. For this purpose dream work may interweave certain materials from waking life, including residuals of the day's experiences, into the content of any particular dream. According to Freud, the process is not arbitrary but depends very much upon the operations of certain mechanisms that will create the most satisfactory dream under the circumstances in which the dreamer finds himself.

The basic mechanism of dream work is that of *representation*, through which wishes emerge into the content of the dream. *Displacement* is another important mechanism that disguises the obvious characteristics of the wish. The close interplay between representation and displacement creates symbols that are manifested in the dream but that will not disturb sleep. Freud postulated the action of a *censor*, a faculty of the unconscious mind that controls the selection of representational elements through displacement.

Not only does a symbol emerge through dream work as a working compromise between assertion and disguise, but the symbol emerges also as an element of multiple meanings. This is accomplished through the mechanism of *condensation*. Freud felt that often a great deal of latent meaning was condensed into one or two dream symbols.

A final stage of dream work, comparable to editing a manuscript, is that of *secondary elaboration*. The process involved continues into the dreamer's efforts to recall and report dreams.

Freud's system of dream interpretation normally calls for a deep psychoanalysis of the dreamer. The interpreter is rarely sure of having achieved a "rock bottom" meaning for a dream even after prolonged analysis. The process is long and difficult and far from absolute. Erik Erikson has demonstrated the depths of psychoanalytic dream interpretation by probing more deeply into one of Freud's dreams (the Irma dream) than Freud himself did.

Wish-fulfillment theory, while perhaps valid in a limited way, appears in the eyes of many critics too narrow a construct for understanding the function of the dream. Freud has been criticized for giving too little credence to the importance of the manifest dream, for underemphasizing its representational features while overemphasizing its disguise features. Finally, he has also been criticized for possibly overemphasizing the function of the dream as the protector of sleep. For some people at least, the dream seems rather to serve as a warning system that all is not well in the dreamer or in his environment. People in dangerous situations often are signaled into a waking alertness of specific dangers by their dreams.

Carl Jung took issue with Sigmund Freud's position on the dream. Jung maintained that Freud actually underestimated the importance of the dream. The unconscious, Jung maintained, presents a truer picture of what the individual is than does waking consciousness, and the dream is the specific expression of the unconscious. According to Jung, Freud in his analytic practice took the dream only as a beginning point from which the dreamer, through free association, rambled onward into the various recesses of his personality, eventually to unravel his neurosis. Jung suggested that almost any statement or idea of the dreamer could serve the same starting-point function.

Jung's approach was more explicitly that of taking the dream both as a starting point and as an end point in order to exhaust the meaning of the dream, *per se*. What is revealed in the dream is capable of restoring balance between the human conscious and unconscious. The dream for Jung does not deny or disguise but asserts and expresses the most basic of man's needs and conflicts. During sleep, then, the dream amplifies rather than disguises man's problems.

For Jung, sex was only one of several important things which might express themselves in dreams. Downgrading the significance of sex, Jung also denied wish fulfillment, censorship, and the dream as guardian of sleep.

Jung also went further than Freud in trying to determine the psychological significance of dream symbolism. Among Jung's contributions to dream theory was the development of the concept of archetypal images. No precise definitions have been given, either by Jung or by adherents to his theory, for the archetypes. The concept evokes less than enthusiastic acceptance from many people, not simply because it lacks precision but because a mystical haze seems to surround it.

There has been some tendency to interpret Jung's concept of the archetypes as the transmission through the species of images acquired in man's long evolutionary experience. Certainly a more acceptable interpretation of what Jung meant by archetypal images is that they result from common biological and psychological functions in the human species. The *images* are not inherited, but man's *potential* for forming such images may be the result of a common human inheritance.

Jung asked as much about what the dream seemed to be pointing to as he did about the origin of the dream. He felt that archetypes not only represent a residual from past human experience but that they also have significance for the present and future situations of dreamers. He saw the dream not as a divinatory experience but as the representation of a directed psychological force seeking fruition in waking activities. In this sense, the dream has cultural and social implications marking the advance of the culture and of the species as well as of the individual. In short, the dream may be man's way of probing into new ideas, engaging in speculation about what can be done to better his condition, and practicing for successful performances in waking life.

For Freud, the dream was analogous to a shade darkening the psyche. For Jung, the dream was analogous to a mirror reflecting human potential as well as human actuality. Freud saw the dream as a somewhat disturbed state of psychological activity pointing in the direction of poor mental health. Jung saw the dream as a normal and even creative state of mental activity expressive of health as well as pathology.

Alfred Adler agreed with Jung on two important points: that dreams should be considered from a purposive as well as a causal perspective, and that symbols can be interpreted accurately only from the context of the meta-phorical content of a given dream.

Adler believed that the purpose of the dream is the solution of the dreamer's personal problems. Rarely, however, are problems clearly mani-fested either in the dream or in waking life since in both states people resort to self-deception to shield themselves from the more painful aspects of their problems. Adler, therefore, agreed with Freud that the latent properties of the dream—having to do with problem solution—are often obscured by manifest symbolism, hiding the dreamer's motivations and the true nature of his problems.

For an understanding of the dream, Adler looked more to its emotional context and its metaphorical pattern than he did to its discrete symbolism. Because dreams represent a need for powerful, but painful, emotions to assert themselves, it is functional for the dream to be shrouded in the mystery of obscure symbolism. Dream solutions do not necessarily require consciousness. To Adler, it seemed that some problems could be solved at the unconscious level without the dreamer's awareness of the problem or its solution.

Once interpreted, dreams can reveal much about an individual's particular style of life. Adler believed that each individual develops a unique style of life for solving personal problems. Although mechanisms of problem solution are different in the waking and sleeping mind, an individual solves his problems in dreams in a way compatible with his particular life style. If because of extreme self-deception in waking life a person fails to maintain his basic life style, Adler asserted that it becomes the purpose of the dream to help an individual defend a healthy style of life against wakeful experiences which threaten it. Despite the ambiguity of the dream because of the essentially deceptive character of dream symbolism, Adler expressed the paradox that the dream might more clearly than wakeful life reveal an individual's style of life.

We are indebted to both Jung and Adler for accenting the positive features of dream experience. Both theorists outline the problem-solving and creative functions of the dream. Both theorists attribute ego-oriented reality-like functions to the dream, a formulation absent in Freud's theory.

Erich Fromm, using the theories of Freud and Jung as points of departure, makes a further theoretical statement on dreaming, which he sees as a symbolic and universal language. In this language, feelings and thoughts are expressed as though they are sensory experiences or events in the world of wakefulness. As do the other theorists, Fromm concedes to the dream a logic that differs from the logic of wakefulness. As a language, the dream has its own syntax and grammar.

Fromm maintains that dream language has been forgotten by modern man, but that modern man can and should relearn this universal idiom. A dream is understood as an important message from the dreamer to himself.

W. H. R. Rivers, a British neurologist who became an ethnologist, took an interest in the dream which helped direct, at least temporarily, the attentions of some British anthropologists of the 1920s and 1930s toward the dreams of preliterate peoples. Rivers argued that dreams are chiefly representative of attempts to solve in sleep personal conflicts which are disturbing and unresolved in waking life. In this argument he added one more voice to the growing life of theorists who postulated problem-solving properties in the dream.

Key words to understanding recent developments in dream theory are "cognition" and "continuity." One can trace, as a general movement in dream theory from Freud to those who came after him, an increasing focus on the revealing aspects of the dream and a perception of a more continuous bond between primary and secondary manifestations of dream thought. An example of this movement within psychoanalysis itself is to be found in the work of Thomas French and Erika Fromm. These authors, using what they call a systematic but intuitive approach to a psychoanalytic understanding of the dream, have found that the thought processes underlying dreams are much better organized than they were previously assumed to be. Dream meanings appear to fit into an intelligible cognitive structure and to be clearly related to situations in the waking life of the dreamer at the time he experiences his dreams. The manifest content of dreams figures prominently in the dreamer's cognitive assessment of his life situation and accordingly reflects continuity between life situation and dream experience.

Frederick Perls, who identified himself as a Gestalt therapist, saw the dream as an existential message informing the dreamer where he is in relation to himself and the world about him at any given time. In group-therapy sessions, dreamers use their dreams to progress along what Perls called the "royal road to integration." Dreams are literally acted out by dreamers who take oppositional or conflictual positions on outstanding images in their dreams. In this way they learn to experience the significance of these images as points of conflict and alienation within the personality. The more fragmented elements in personality are brought into harmony with the whole. Through interpretive dream analysis, the dream is vitalized in wakefulness and in social context to facilitate the growth of the individual. The manifest elements of the dream are accepted as cognitively significant and therefore reflective of the dreamer's life situation.

While the approach of Calvin Hall toward understanding the dream is essentially different from the approach of Frederick Perls, there appears to be an underlying agreement in their theoretical assessments. Hall has collected thousands of written reports of their dreams from normal and abnormal persons from all walks of life, from people of both sexes and all ages. Hall is basically interested in the cognitive properties of dreams, which he feels are revealed in the manifest content of dreams. Also, Hall maintains that there is a basic continuity between waking life and dream experience. He argues that people are essentially the same whether they are awake or asleep.

More vehemently perhaps than anyone else, Hall criticizes the theory of opposite meanings in dreams, the interpretation that good luck means bad luck, that love means hate, and the like. He asserts that the wishes and fears which inform our waking life and give shape to our actions also determine in large measure what we dream about. Hall's research indicates that we do not dream of everything from waking life. Those things that preoccupy us rather than occupy us take on prominence in our dreams.

Recent developments in dream theory and experimentation have emphasized the importance of the manifest *content* of the dream. One theorist, Richard Jones, however, seeks to include as well an emphasis on the manifest *structure* of the dream. Strongly oriented toward the psychoanalytic school of dream interpretation, Jones nevertheless feels that Freud failed to take into consideration functions within the dream relating to ego synthesis and the gradual unfolding of the personality with maturation. This deficiency Jones seeks to remedy. Jones indicates that it is feasible to study the adaptive and reality-orientation aspects of the dream through manifest structure as well as through manifest content. He uses a method of analysis that follows the conceptual scheme of Erik Erikson with regard to personality development over a number of stages extending from infancy into maturity. The personality of the dreamer becomes increasingly more complex on the basis of maturational determinants and environmental experiences; the change, Jones believes, should become apparent in manifest dream structure and content.

Testing Hypotheses of Dream Function

More and more, it seems, dream researchers are becoming interested in testing hypotheses relating to how the dream functions, rather than in simply drawing after-the-fact conclusions about observations they have made. One such hypothesis and some empirical work connected with it is reported here.

Freud thought that the basic needs associated with hunger and thirst would be relatively directly expressed in manifest dream content. As basic tissue needs, thwarted by the reality of waking life, hunger and thirst can be assumed, according to Freudian theory, to give rise to impulses or wishes expressed in dreams. Freud felt that these impulses would not be so heavily disguised by the censor as would sexual impulses, for instance, simply because culture customarily places fewer restrictions on the satisfaction of needs for food and drink than on the satisfaction of sexual needs. Freud cites, in his writing, a few examples of the relatively direct expression of hunger motivation in the manifest dream.

Otto Nordenskjold and Gunnar Anderson reported that when food supplies were low in an Antarctic expedition meat and drink were the centers around which the dreams of their personnel revolved. A member of their party who made a specialty of attending dream banquets was particularly pleased one morning to relate that he ate through three courses before awakening. Observers of people in extreme situations of food deprivation have reported similar anecdotal material.

Allan Holmberg, an anthropologist who worked among the Sirionó of Bolivia, reports that their supply of food is always insecure. In wakefulness, the Sirionó have almost an obsession with food. Holmberg found that themes of eating, hunting game, and collecting edible plant foods from their forest environment were found in over 50 percent of the dream narratives he collected from them. Holmberg is not so sure that dreams of food are responses to immediate tissue requirements, but rather that the food dream represents a generalized response to the environment indicating that hunger is one of the most intense motivating forces in Sirionó society.

Controlled and laboratory research indicates no simple or direct relationship between tissue needs in hunger and thirst and clear expressions of these needs in dream experience. A small-scale empirical study on the effects of hunger on the dreams of American males was conducted by F. G. Benedict and his associates in 1919. The results were weak but positive in indicating that dreams gave evidence of the tissue needs associated with hunger. Another study conducted on conscientious-objector volunteers during World War II by Ancel Keys and his associates was essentially negative in linking hunger to expressions of food imagery and eating in dreams. This research was a generally fine study of the biology of human starvation under controlled conditions. That part of the study, however, which looked at the effects of semistarvation on dreams appears to have been an afterthought in the minds of the investigators. The investigators apparently expected to see some kind of direct relationship between food deprivation and food imagery in dreams. This expectation, coupled with an inadequate methodology in collecting and assessing the dream data, contributed to the essentially negative findings of that study.

Tissue needs for liquids also are not necessarily expressed directly in the manifest content of the dream. Two University of Chicago dream researchers, William Dement and Edward Wolpert, collected fifteen dreams from three thirsty subjects in a laboratory situation. Five of the fifteen dreams revealed thirst-related content. The investigators concluded that the physiological condition of thirst does not appear to have a strong influence on manifest dream content. No doubt these investigators, as have others, expected to find a virtual one-to-one relationship between physical thirst and its psychological expression in dreams.

Working on a Ph.D. dissertation at New York University, Edwin Bokert deprived 18 subjects of food and drink for the eight hours prior to their coming to the sleep laboratory, where they were fed a highly spiced meal. Later, as they slept, a tape recorder repeated the phrase, "a cool delicious drink of water," over and over within the auditory range of the sleepers. Bokert found that the thirst of his subjects became manifest in their reported dreams which were collected through the night. The general finding was that dreams of liquids increased during the experiment; some dreamers even incorporated the taped phrase into their manifest dreams.

Perhaps most interesting in the light of Freudian theory was the finding that subjects who had dreamed of satisfying their thirst actually drank less upon awakening than did subjects who dreamed only of being thirsty. The finding suggests that the satisfaction of thirst in their dreams in some way relieved the actual thirst of the subjects. In Freud's terminology, primary-process thinking associated with the content of dream fantasy actually seemed to function in terms of need satisfaction or "wish" fulfillment, which Freud perceived as the basic function of the dream.

Intrigued with this basic Freudian hypothesis, I (Carl O'Nell) did research on the influence of hunger and thirst on the manifest dream content of people from four cultural settings. The data did not lend themselves to any exact measure of tissue need on the part of the dreamers. The data did, however, specify whether any group was fasting or nonfasting at the time of dream collection. Knowledge about the significance of the fast for the fasting groups, knowledge about attitudes toward food and drink intake for all the groups, and an understanding of the general dietary practices of all the groups comprised the essential data available to the researcher.

As investigator I found that it was possible, using reported dreams, to render a judgment about the presence or absence of food frustration for each group. Each judgmental category was defined as a food-frustration component. A positive judgment on a given component for any group was scored as 1 for that group. Similarly, a negative judgment on a given component for any group was scored as 0 for that group. Component scores were summed for each group. Groups were then ranked on the basis of total food-frustration scores.

The six components of food frustration used in the study were the following. Component one was concerned with whether or not the group in question was undergoing a formalized fast at the time of dream collection. Component two required a judgment based on ethnographic data about the relative intensity, prolongation, or frequency of the fasting experience for each group. Component three involved a judgment, again based on ethnographic data for each group, about the stringency of the enforced sanctions which accompanied the fast. Component four concerned ethnographic data relating to whether or not there were negative food proscriptions (such as well-defined food taboos) other than fasting for any of the groups. Component five was concerned with evidence that the people in any group might be suffering the effects of chronic undernutrition. Component six was concerned with evidence that the people in any of the groups under study might be suffering the effects of malnutrition.

Dreams in the study were from the following groups: Ethiopian Orthodox Christians, fasting Nigerian Muslims, nonfasting Nigerians, and nonfasting Americans. All dreamers were male students of approximately the same age.

The total dream sample consisted of two dream reports from each of 434 students.

The Ethiopian Orthodox Christians achieved a food frustration score of 5; the fasting Nigerians, a score of 3; the nonfasting Nigerians, a score of 1; and the Americans a score of 0. Of the four groups, it was assumed that the Ethiopians were experiencing the most intense hunger motivation, while the Americans were experiencing the least intense hunger motivation.

Ethiopian Orthodox Christians practice some of the most stringent of fasts. Children begin to fast from age 7 and fasting expectations increase with age and elevation to higher status. A typical adult layman fasts approximately 165 days of the year.

The fasting Nigerians, mostly Hausa, were observing the fast of Ramadan at the time their dreams were reported. The fast from food and drink is complete in the daylight hours. Fasting is a public issue and strictly observed. Social pressure to keep the fast is great and fasting appears to be the last religious practice that a wayward Muslim will discard.

The nonfasting Nigerians, mostly Ibo and Yoruba, were judged positive on only one food-frustration component, that of malnutrition. Their diet was judged to be low in protein relative to a high intake of carbohydrates. Although not undernourished, because their overall food intake in terms of calories is high, the nonfasting Nigerians nevertheless fit the United Nations Food and Agriculture Organization's criterion of malnutrition which applies when more than two-thirds of the diet is composed of roots, grains, and sugars.

In comparison with the others, the Americans were judged not to be deficient in their diets; the American goal of a balanced diet is not lost even on adolescents. The American students, as a group, were not assumed to have been suffering any appreciable amount of food frustration, especially since they were from middle and upper-middle social strata. As a cultural item, fasting was of no significance for the American group.

It was predicted then, on the basis of their food-frustration scores, that the Ethiopians would have a higher level of food-related imagery in their dreams than would the fasting Nigerians, who in turn would be higher than the nonfasting Nigerians, who would be higher than the Americans. The hypothesis was strongly confirmed. By the measure of manifest dream content set up for study, 63.8 percent of the Ethiopians, 43.8 percent of the fasting Nigerians, 33.7 percent of the nonfasting Nigerians and 14.5 percent of the Americans indicated manifest hunger in their dreams.

Thirst was judged to be a factor which, because of the Ramadan prohibition against drinking in the daylight hours, separated the fasting Nigerians from all other groups in the sample. In support of the hypothesis put forward by the investigator, thirst-related imagery was found to be significantly higher in the dreams of the fasting Nigerians than it was for any of the other groups. Of the drink-deprived Nigerians, 19 percent showed manifest thirst in their dreams as compared to 10 percent of the other groups combined.

Calvin Hall has informed me, in personal communication, that the percentage of food imagery found in the dreams of Americans in this study is consistent with percentages of food imagery he has found in the reported dreams of very large and general samples of American dreamers.

What implications can we draw for the function of the dream from the findings of this study? First of all, it would probably be erroneous to assume that the higher percentages of manifest food imagery in the dreams of the Ethiopians and the fasting Nigerians were due primarily to tissue needs in the dreamers. Secondly, it would probably be almost as fallacious to assume that the higher food-imagery scores can be attributed primarily to social and cultural conditions attending food frustration for these groups. The most reasonable interpretation would seem to be that both physiological and sociocultural factors combine with other factors, primarily of a psychological nature, to define for the dreamers needs that are expressed differentially in the manifest content of dreams. The measures of food imagery found in the dreams are certainly measures of psychological experience. By the same token, it would seem that the measures of food frustration also are to be psychologically defined. A psychological need, created in whole or in part by physiological and sociocultural conditions, becomes psychologically expressed in dreams. Unless physiological and sociocultural factors become psychologically relevant to dreamers, these factors are not likely to be expressed in their dreams.

The anthropologist Robert Munroe and his associates studied the effects of population density on concerns with food in three East African societies: the Logoli, the Gusii, and the Kipsigis of Kenya. Of the three groups the most densely populated is that of the Logoli. The Kipsigis is the least densely populated group, and the Gusii fall roughly in between the other two in population density. Because their food technologies and economies are comparable, Munroe postulated a more intense concern with food by the most densely populated group than he did for either of the less densely populated groups. Using the content of folk tales as cultural measures of food concern, Munroe expected to find evidence of relatively great food concern among the Logoli, somewhat less concern among the Gusii, and the least amount of food concern among the Kipsigis. His findings matched his expectations.

Munroe then used other measures of food concern, such as psychologically projected food themes in the responses of 333 adolescent students from each of the three groups. The students were asked to respond to stories which were presented to them for their interpretations. Once again his hypothesis was supported.

With these cultural and psychological measures of food concern supporting his general hypothesis that greater population pressure would create greater food concern among culturally similar groups, Munroe then went to the use of manifest dream content. He did so to test the hypothesis that groups with demonstrably greater concern about food in daily life experience would reflect this concern in their dreams. Surprisingly, the investigators came up with a reverse finding. Only 12 percent of Logoli students dreamed of eating, whereas 20 percent of Gusii students and 30 percent of Kipsigis students dreamed of eating.

Just why, in the light of dream theory and in the presence of empirical evidence provided from other studies (such as the one I conducted), societies with obvious food concerns in waking life would not express these concerns more openly and more frequently at the manifest level of dreams is not clear. Certainly the physical and cultural exigencies contributing to food concern make that concern psychologically relevant. Munroe's psychological measures demonstrate this relevance.

Two things seem to be at work here. One of them is suggested by general Freudian dream theory. Food concern at the cultural and more overt psychological levels may create anxiety over that food concern which serves to disguise it at the manifest level of dream experience. In Freudian language, food concern may be expressed more at the latent than at the manifest level for the more anxious groups.

It seems more likely that a second possible factor at work here may be the one responsible for the Munroe *et al.* findings. The second factor has to do with the measures used by these investigators. Munroe suggests that the measure they used might have been too narrow to reflect the breadth of food concern. They used only the manifest measure of eating food. The fasting/nonfasting study used a broad measure of food-related concern. On this basis the two studies are not strictly comparable.

The Salience of the Psychological Function

Laboratory work, in general, has demonstrated that both presleep stimuli and stimuli applied to subjects during sleep have effects on dream content. Such content, however, usually emerges as a transformed manifestation of an original stimulus. Experiences of previous-day activities, normally with strong visual components, appear to be incorporated in some recognizable way into 25 to 50 percent of dreams reported in the laboratory. Sensory stimuli relating to the senses of touch, taste, and smell, when such stimuli are applied to the dreamer in sleep, are manifestly incorporated into dreams from 10 to 25 percent of the time. As yet, the rates of incorporation of stimuli arising spontaneously within the organism have not been assessed.

It seems obvious that not all stimuli, nor all experiences in daily life, enter the world of dreams. Calvin Hall, for one, has emphasized the conceptual over the perceptual functions of the dream. In other words, the dream appears not simply to register in perception the experiences from either the inner or outer world of the dreamer, but rather to interpret and organize the range of such experiences into a conceptual framework psychologically meaningful to the dreamer.

The answer to the question of what dreams do (that is, how they function) rests in large part on an understanding of how the dream reflects human needs which have achieved psychological salience for dreamers. We may speak of the cultural, social, and biological functions of dreams. But it is increasingly clear that cultural, social, and biological factors must be transformed into meaningful psychological factors before they can emerge as manifest elements in the organization of dream thought. Whatever processes govern the psychological mechanisms of dreaming, there appears to be a gatekeeping function among them which selectively determines which elements in a dreamer's life experience will enter the dream.

Studying connections between various types of stimuli and dream content is an essential first step in the direction of uncovering answers relating to dream function. In taking this step we must consider those psychological dispositions in dreamers that mediate between stimuli and content. While the dream may serve physiological, social, and cultural functions, these functions rest upon the more salient psychological functions.

5

CULTURAL AND SOCIAL
DREAM FUNCTIONS

Because the dream is a universal human experience, it impels man to give it a cultural definition. As we have seen, not all cultures attribute equal significance to the dream. Largely because of this differing significance, dreams often have somewhat different functions in different cultures.

The dream appears to have five different cultural and social functions. Since these five functions are not mutually exclusive, the dream may be seen to function in any or all of the five ways in any given culture.

It seems, first, that dream experience may be more or less directly translated into cultural experience; the dream functions as a direct input into culture. Second, the dreams of individuals may be used to facilitate the solving of cultural or social problems experienced by the group; in this context the dream may serve either maintenance or innovative functions. Third, the dream may function to define status for individuals, legitimizing one's cultural participation in possibly unique, but more often in ordinary, ways; this same basic function of the dream may simply extend cultural support to individual needs. Fourth, the dream may serve in the maintenance of social control; the content of the dream will be interpreted in such a way as to lend support to prescribed behaviors while it censors proscribed behaviors. The fifth function of the dream is to facilitate social-psychological adjustment; and because the dream in all cultures reflects certain psychological effects of cultural participation it is possible to make use of dreams for studying differences in cultural affiliation.

Dreams Contribute to Culture

Human dreams have given rise to systems for explaining human experience and behavior. Dreams have what has been called a *scopophilic* quality.

57

In psychological and particularly psychoanalytic literature, scopophilia defines a desire to look at sexually stimulating scenes particularly as a substitute for actual sexual participation. Many dreams are scopophilic in that sexual motivation is frequently expressed in manifest dream content. However, in a more general sense, scopophilia as reflected in dreams implies that the dreamer stands somewhat apart from the scenes he experiences in his dreams. In this more general sense of the term probably most dreams are scopophilic.

It is in this detachment, a characteristic of dreams that permits the dreamer to stand aside from his dream experience and view the workings of his mind in a more or less neutral way, that we have an interest here. This scopophilic quality of dreams, which often makes the dreamer feel as though he is a spectator not very directly involved in the action of his dreams, may have had far-reaching cultural consequences in man's evolutionary development. In dreams, the organism appears to the dreamer to be divisible into parts: the passive resting body and the active observing mind. For this reason, dream experience is conducive to an interpretive separation of body and mind.

Sir Edward Tylor, a British anthropologist of the nineteenth century, developed the theory that the scopophilic quality of dreams (he did not use the term) induced many preliterate peoples to believe, on the basis of their dreams, that individuals are composed of corporeal and spiritual elements. In sleep and dreaming, accordingly, the spiritual element roams about apart from the body to interact with other spirits and bodies. A more generalized belief holds that many features of the natural environment also are composed of material and spiritual elements. This belief, called animism, is a central part of the religious belief systems of many preliterate peoples. Thus Tylor saw dream experience as an important contributor to the development of primitive religious thought.

Animism, associated with dream belief, is exemplified by the Andaman Islanders studied by the British anthropologist A. R. Radcliffe-Brown. In Andaman belief, each person has a double or spirit counterpart to his physical being. One evidence for the double is the reflection one can see of oneself in a clear pond. Dreams are explained by saying that the sleeper's double is wandering about away from his body. Dreams are interlocked with reality and with the belief in a spiritual world which forms part of that reality. The Andaman Islanders maintain that it is dangerous to awaken someone from sleep because the spiritual double may be so far away from the body that the awakening might bring illness to the body in case the spirit cannot return quickly enough.

The pygmy Negritos of North Central Luzon, studied by the psychologist Kilton Stewart, also have a belief that the spirit wanders about in sleep. The world in which one wanders in sleep is the spiritual world and the dreamer has both the opportunity and obligation to communicate with the beings of that world. The dreamer's experiences, translated into group experience in wake-

ful activity, seemingly give rise to commonly shared beliefs; these, institutionalized and involving more or less set patterns of behavior, become the
magic or religion of a preliterate group. (Anthropologists also have other
theories of preliterate religion and magic that are beyond the scope of a book
dealing with dreams.)

Géza Róheim, a psychoanalyst who became an anthropologist, intensively
studied some of the aboriginal groups of Australia in the early decades of this
century. Róheim's understanding of myth and ritual among the preliterate
Australians rests on his understanding of the dream. He gave a strong
Freudian interpretation to the general idea that the dream life of a people
would give rise to certain cultural developments. He insisted, far more
vehemently than most anthropologists would, that we must understand the
dream in order to understand preliterate culture.

Nevertheless, Róheim's ideas are interesting, and with qualification, may
have some validity. Principally, one must guard against the temptation to
interpret culture in basically psychological terms.

As we fall asleep, according to Róheim, the outer environment holds less
meaning for us, until, fully asleep, we become totally absorbed in the
sensations of our inner experiences. These experiences seem to emanate from
ourselves, in a thought process called projection, to form a new world—the
world of our dreams. In slightly different terms, this is the mechanism that
creates the scopophilic quality of dream experience.

Róheim compares the content of the projected experiences of the body in
sleep, reflected in the dream, with the content of the narratives of the "dream
times" of various Australian aboriginal groups. He concludes that although
there are manifest differences in content between dream experience and
narrative, there is an essential similarity between everyday human psychological experience and cultural product. The manifest elements in myth and
ritual are cultural overlays for dream experiences that have been translated by
any given group into culturally meaningful symbols and behaviors.

In his myths and rituals—according to Róheim—man creates his own
environment. But he does so largely on the basis of his own inner experiences, his dreams. In their ritualistic practices and in the mythologies which
sustain these practices, the Australian aboriginal groups believe, they are
maintaining a continuity with the events of creation which they refer to as
"dream time" (altjeringa, a word used by the Arunta, Kaitish, and Unmatjera
for both dreams and creation.) Many elaborate totemic and initiation rites are
yearly reenactments of creation myths which reinforce the idea of man's
oneness with his environment. But both natural and human environments are
the visible results of man's interaction—in primal times—with the great
creative spirits.

For the Andaman Islanders, the Negrito pygmies, and the Australian
Aborigines, the dream appears to have an "input" into the culture of the

groups. But one does not necessarily have to look at preliterate groups to find a cultural input from dreams. The Buddhist interpretation of the world seems largely to be based on a generalized interpretation of dream experience. One can have a sense of experiencing reality in dreams. Upon awakening, this sense of dream reality normally disappears. But the sense of reality in waking life could be interpreted as yet another dream state from which one can also awaken into still another, and higher, state of reality. Such appears to be the Buddhist concept of reality, that is, a metaphysical concept of degrees of reality based on an amplification of a cultural interpretation of the dream state.

Dreams Sustain Culture

Dreams appear to be not only formative (to some degree) of culture but also supportive of culture among various peoples. That is, dreams help to validate the traditional in culture, serving in support of maintenance systems contributing to cultural continuity. As the anthropologists Alfred Kroeber and George Devereux both point out in consequence of their work with the Mojave Indians, the dream is made to serve the purposes of validating the traditional in culture and of screening items of cultural innovation. Even though, ostensibly, the dream was conceived of differently by the Iroquois and by the Mojave, a deep function of the dream in both societies was that of cultural maintenance. Dreams were interpreted in both cultural systems in ways to conserve the basic values of the cultural systems.

As input into the cultural system, the dream is not always accepted in the form in which it is experienced or originally reported by the individual dreamer. One type of alteration mechanism has already been touched on for the Mae Enga of New Guinea. Dreams are sometimes "tailored" by the group before they can serve the functions of cultural input or maintenance.

The modification is not always a conscious process on the part of the peoples involved. A dream may undergo considerable modification in its telling and retelling to a number of people before it reaches some stage of cultural input. Cora DuBois, an anthropologist who studied the culture and psychological adjustment of the Alorese, who inhabit a small jungle island in Indonesia, has indicated how dreams customarily undergo revision in the telling process. Dreams are culturally relevant for the Alorese in that they are considered to be meaningful human experiences. A dreamer impressed with his own dream will regularly awaken other members of the household to report a dream he has just experienced. Such dreams are not simply reported, but animatedly discussed. DuBois believes that in the telling, discussion, and retelling of dreams a considerable amount of cultural material comes to be interwoven into the dreams.

According to Dorothy Eggan, Hopi dreams were often woven into what she called "dream stories." A dream story consists of an end product of dream experience and the dreamer's associations to that experience, involving cultural interpretations of the dream. Eggan maintains that there is an interaction between the manifest dream and the belief and value systems of the culture. The deities of the Hopi dreamer's culture take on an added dimension of reality for him in waking life because he dreams about them. Dreams often bring into focus conflict situations over inappropriate behaviors in waking life. The dreamer reads cultural meaning into his dream and, after assessing dream experience in terms of cultural meaning, will often modify his behavior in waking life. Inappropriate waking-life behaviors become recognizable in the dream against a backdrop of cultural interpretation, after which such behaviors are generally abandoned or modified in waking life.

Dreams Facilitate Cultural Innovation

The dream helps to facilitate human problem solving and the cultural innovation this implies. The Mojave creation myth, which validates cultural elaboration and change, is continually being added to by the dreams of Mojave shamans. George Devereux indicates that gunshot wounds, and most importantly the cure for them, became part of the Mojave creation myth after the introduction of firearms into Mojave culture. He predicts the possible incorporation of radiation and space illnesses, and their cures, into the Mojave creation myth if these things eventually emerge as possible innovations in Mojave culture.

Adapting new and viable life styles as a result of cultural contact is an imperative faced by many traditional cultures in the modern world. Often a new cultural trait will emerge as an amalgamation of old and new cultural elements.

Dreams were of significance to the traditional culture of the Kashia Pomo of California. Dreams have emerged as the basis for a religious cult among the Kashia Pomo that represents a complex between the old and the new. The dream cult, which is as much new as old, stands as a revitalization movement giving force and meaning to the current culture.

The dream-cult leader, or shaman, is an official dreamer. Her dreams are taken as indications from the spirit world of what is proper in interpersonal and ritual behavior. Sacred symbols in the content of her dreams are reproduced in material objects such as dream canes, banners, and flags used in the rituals of the cult. Some of the symbols to emerge in dreams are recognizable for their significance in the broader context of American culture, symbols such as the stars and stripes of the American flag and the cross of Christianity.

Rituals based on dreams have apparently had adaptive value, both for the group and individuals in it. The Pomo believe that special dances, based on dreams of the shaman during World War II, were instrumental in the safe return of Pomo soldiers. The power of these dances is currently invoked by anyone facing danger. The dream affords psychological security to believers. At the social and cultural levels, it functions to forestall social disintegration and to facilitate gradual cultural change.

Cultural change may be either facilitated or impeded by the dream. Among the Basuto of Africa, people traditionally expected to receive dream messages about important actions to be undertaken in wakefulness. Although an individual Basuto might be positively disposed toward a personal acceptance of Christianity (a fairly common situation in the early decades of this century), most people waited for an indication to conversion to be given them in their dreams. Lacking such an indication, a person on the verge of conversion would refuse baptism until such an indication would manifest itself in his dreams.

The effect of cultural change prompted by dreams might in some cases be so innovative that the result seems to reflect little or nothing of the cultures in contact. Datu Bintung, an influential dreamer among the Senoi of Malaya, effected such a cultural change through his dreams. An important feature of one of Datu Bintung's dreams was the elevation of the ceremonial status of women to a level near that of men in Senoi society. The dream contained a stipulation to equality which was accompanied by a concrete "gift" to the people in the form of a dance which exemplified the equality. This movement toward greater sexual equality was not a reflection of traditional Senoi values or practices, nor was it reflective of male/female status relations in either the Islamic or Chinese societies in contact with the Senoi. It seems to have been a creative social product emerging from the dream experience of an influential leader.

In some cases the function of the dream is to bring into operation mechanisms associated with the normal institutional structures of society. The changes in these cases are not radical departures from tradition but are in the nature of dynamic movements characteristic of all viable social forms.

For the Iroquois, the dream appearance of a cultural hero often became a matter of national concern. Chiefs came together to confer with one another. Clairvoyants were called in to probe the full significance of the dream. Councils were arranged for large-scale discussions. Discussions included a broad spectrum of affairs, often centered on the most practical problems confronting the group. Intense effort was made to determine how best to satisfy the wishes of the dream spirit. In these decision-making processes involved in attempting to satisfy the wishes of the spirit, solutions were forthcoming which often met urgent needs of the group. The dream in this case functioned to instigate at the group level a problem-solving process that utilized normal social mechanisms but that did not necessarily call for radical cultural innovation.

Cultural Dreams and the Individual

One sociocultural function of the dream is to help define status for an individual. Another such function, related to it, is that of providing an individual with sociocultural support at some critical point in life.

Among the Paviotso Indians of Nevada, a man or woman could achieve the status of shaman by having the proper dream experience. According to the anthropologist Willard Park, dreams conferring the status of shaman upon an individual could either be sought or unsought. Unsought dreams were of two types. One type of dream bringing power to a shaman was that of an animal which would appear to the dreamer a great number of times, repeatedly announcing to the dreamer that he was to become a shaman and informing him in the curing arts, especially teaching him the necessary curative songs. Another type of dream was that about a dead ancestor from the previous generation who had shamanistic powers. The ancestor would appear, as did the animal, both to inform the dreamer of his selection to shamanistic status and to instruct him in the arts of his calling. When the animal or the image of the deceased relative ceased to appear in an individual's dreams it was assumed that he had received the full powers of his calling.

It was considered dangerous for a person to disregard dreams indicating he had been selected by the spirits to become a shaman. The disregard of such dreams would eventuate in death. Dreams not only had the power to bring health and life to an individual, but also had the power to bring illness and death. Dreams were used by curing specialists to diagnose the causes of illness, to control illness, and to restore health.

An individual who had not received a call from the spirit world to become a shaman might nevertheless beseech the spirit world to grant him this power. The power, needless to say, gave him enhanced social status within his group. The supplicant would often seek such power by obtaining visions in caves. The visions were interpreted in much the same way as were dreams. Night dreams conferring shamanistic status normally followed having these visions.

Dreams bringing similar vocations to special power and prestige for an individual have been reported for cultures from virtually every culture area in the world. Although the details of how the dream mediates between the culture and the individual may vary somewhat from culture to culture, the broad function of using the dream as a device for elevating individuals to special status is fairly consistent across cultural boundaries.

Dreams can also serve as means of providing an individual with socio-cultural support in critical life situations. Cultures which link an individual or a group to a guardian spirit in dreams characteristically employ this dream function. Recall what was said about guardian-spirit dreams of the North American Indians and the Sea Dyaks in an earlier section.

In some cultures, the dreamer builds a special relationship with the spiritual world. In other cultures, the dream permits the dreamer to build special relations with his waking-life fellows.

The use of dreams among the Naskapi Indians of Labrador is an example of the individual using his dreams to build a special relationship with the spiritual world. The Naskapi are simple hunters who live in small, isolated family units in a harsh physical environment. This cultural group has neither elaborate customs nor ceremonies to sustain group values. It also has very little by way of collective religious belief.

The individual Naskapi hunter's life is marked by solitude. In being enculturated into his group, he has had to learn to rely for survival on his inner psychological resources as well as his own physical resources. He sees his inner self, or soul, as his most important life companion. His soul, which he may call "Great Man," or simply "Friend," is immortal. In its immortality the soul acquires great knowledge and power. At death, the Great Man transfers itself from one individual to another in reincarnation. The continuous life of the soul is the seat of continuing wisdom and strength.

In life, the individual Naskapi seeks to attune himself to the Great Man within himself. He does this by attending to the meaning of his dreams. Being in touch with the Great Man through dreams makes a person more completely human and helps him to be more successful in living his life. In short, the use of the dream in this way by the Naskapi is a mechanism for extending sociocultural support to the individual in the absence of other mechanisms.

One use of dreams among the Iroquois illustrates how dreams were sometimes used in a sociocultural way to establish or reinforce social bonds among individuals. The dreams of a sick person were sometimes interpreted as the dreamer's wanting or needing a friend. Occasionally a specific person would be dreamed of by the sick individual.

During ceremonies conducted by the Eagle Society among the Iroquois, sick persons were matched with friends suggested by their dreams. The friendships thus established implied lifelong relationships between the matched individuals characterized by mutual helpfulness and regard.

From the Naskapi and Iroquois examples, we can observe how the dream has been culturally defined to extend support to the individual.

In all cultures, illness is a problem which calls for a cultural definition of the sick individual's situation, what the nature of the illness is, and how it might be dealt with in cultural context. Some cultures use the dream in one or another or all three approaches to the problems of illness.

The idea that disease can be diagnosed by dreams is an old and continuing one in human thought. Hippocrates and Aristotle made it an explicit theory. It was also an hypothesis of many naturalistic dream theorists of the nineteenth century including Alfred Maury.

The Greeks, the Romans, and later the early Christians sometimes resorted to induced dreams for diagnostic and curative purposes. Dreams were induced in the temples of the Greek god Asklepios, symbolized by a serpent. Harmless serpents were housed in the temple rooms occupied by dream petitioners. Various rites were performed by the petitioners to put themselves into proper dispositions to have dreams and to be cured.

Early Christian dreamers at sacred shrines saw the patron of the shrine who normally appeared as a great healer in his own right or as a representative of the Divine Healer of all men. In modern Japan, invalids who sleep in the holy shrines of the Boddhisattva Yakushi, the master of healing, often see the healing master in their dreams.

Cultures may respond to universal human needs to perceive healers in dreams. The "healer" appears as one of Jung's archetypes, or universal symbols, seemingly a personification, in fantasy, of man's deep desire for the healing of his many ills.

Both patients and curing shamans contribute their dreams, sometimes induced, in the curing of disorders among the Negrito pygmies. Stewart observed that the dreams of both patients and curers are more complex than ordinary dreams experienced by others, that is, dreams not connected with illness. The dreams of curers and patients are characterized by the visitations of spirit guides who communicate with and assist dreamers. The cooperation among patient and curer and the patient's social group encourages directing and strengthening the patient's natural inner will to health in wakefulness and in sleep.

The Navajo traditionally believe that illness is caused by dreams. Evil dreams can be detected either through their content or through their effects on dreamers. Less serious dreams can be counteracted by the dreamer himself, who with the dawn prays to the spirits as he stands in the doorway of his hogan. More serious dreams are told to a diagnostician, who discerns the cause of the illness and prescribes a cure that is a complicated process also involving the dreams of the curer. Dreams causing illness are matters of social concern. In the curing of illness through dreams, among the Navajo, social processes are sometimes of considerable significance. Some dreams are indicative of social as well as physical or mental disorder.

Susto is a folk illness common to many cultures in Latin America. The general belief is that the illness is caused by an evil spirit who captures the soul of the victim. A common complaint of susto sufferers has to do with sleep and dream disorders. Among the Zapotecs, a cultural group studied by the author (O'Nell), susto sufferers usually claim to see the devil in their dreams. But other dream signs of susto are also possible. "Empty dreams," which the dreamer feels are without content, or dreams that are extraordinarily bizarre or frightening are also indicative of susto. "Empty dreams" are accepted as evidence of the weakness of one's soul or its absence from the body. Curers may make use of these dream signs in diagnosing the condition.

Stereotypic dreams are reported by susto sufferers in Yochib, a Tzeltal Maya-speaking community, according to a personal communication from Robert Harman, an anthropologist who has worked there. Among those people, susto is assumed usually to be caused by a fall. The susto dream will involve the location of the fall but not the actual incident of falling. Dreamers are beckoned to the place of the fall by supernatural beings, guardians of the earth, who mostly appear as attractive Ladinas (girls of Spanish origin), offering gifts of food and clothing to the dreamer. The dreamer, wishing both to advance and accept the gifts and to retreat from the powerful spirit, is torn by his dilemma. A final desire to flee the spot is often accompanied by an inability of the dreamer to do so. The spirits stand guard over the soul until appropriate gifts are offered them in the curing processes. If placated, they do not harm the soul but protect it from demons who would devour it.

We see in these examples how cultures, through their interpretations and uses of dreams, extend psychological and social support to cultural participants who are ill. At the very least these dream mechanisms give culturally meaningful interpretations to illness. Almost as often they would seem to facilitate the curing of individuals.

Dreams and the Maintenance of Social Control

The cultural use of dreams may contribute to group control around sets of shared values. One example of this particular function of the dream has already been indicated for the Mae Enga of New Guinea. The interpretation of dreams, among the Mae Enga, often brings pressure to bear on individuals to conform to one or another cultural expectation.

Dreams can also perform this cultural function for the Philippine Negritos. The Negrito has a serious obligation toward his deceased parent to honor that parent by giving an appropriate funeral feast. The community expects the offspring of the dead person to comply with this obligation within a reasonable length of time. There is a temptation for the offspring to delay such a feast as long as possible. Not only will the feast be expensive and exhaust physical resources, but it will also require the feast giver to form new obligations of indebtedness to his fellows. The more important a person was in life, the more impressive must be the funeral banquet that puts him to rest.

The Negritos expect the dead spirit to return to his group from the time of burial until the funeral feast has been made in his honor. The feast is never held until the ghost has made several visits to his offspring in dreams. The ghost instructs his offspring and makes some agreement with him concerning the size and timing of the feast.

Ogong, a young man described by Kilton Stewart, whose important father had died, had not been able to collect the resources necessary for his father's funeral feast. After repeated dream visits from his father, he became so ashamed and terrified that he was unable to sleep. Almost in a trancelike state from loss of sleep when Stewart met him, he willingly submitted to hypnosis. In the full trance, Ogong's father made known his desires, and Ogong (and Stewart) negotiated with him for a proper feast, which was soon held and which released Ogong from the almost nightly visits of his importuning father.

Not all messages from the world of dreams support the generally held values of the people. Again among the Philippine Negritos, it was possible for a person to dream of an antisocial act that he would attempt to carry out in wakefulness. (In general, the Negritos attempt to comply with the manifest messages of their dreams.) But if "dream giants" instructed a Negrito, in a nightmare, to carry out an act tabooed by society, the dreamer met with severe opposition from the elders. In these cases, elders refused to support the "dream giants," whom they usually respected and whom they saw as normal supporters of their values. They might go so far as to "attack," through magic or other means, the "dream giants" who impelled people to perform violent or antisocial actions against the rest of the group. Ultimately, it seems, social-reinforcement dreams would be used against antisocial dreams to force compliance in expected behavior.

Dreams are used in Senoi society to help reinstate in the good graces of others an individual who has behaved in an antisocial way or who has committed a social blunder. Stewart offers the example of a young man who shares with his friends some gourd seeds which he has brought back from the jungle. The seeds act as a purgative and everyone suffers diarrhea as a result of eating them. The young man also suffers great social embarrassment. But the spirit of the gourd seeds comes to him in a dream and reveals that the seeds are not food but medicine to be taken only in illness. Also, the spirit teaches the youth a new song and dance which he can perform for his friends upon awakening. The explanation of the dream and the gift of the spirit help the dreamer to reestablish his position of esteem within the group that he had inadvertently offended.

In many societies, functionaries who serve as arbiters of the moral order are called to their position by dreams. They may also control the moral and social actions of others on the authority of the dreams they have, once they have achieved their special status.

The Korekore Shona of the Zambesi Valley in Rhodesia are one such group. They have an elaborate shamanistic religion which serves as a moral counterpart to the political structure that defines legal regulations. Their institutions are described in a recent book by I. M. Lewis called *Ecstatic Religion*. The shamans are believed to be incarnate spirits of long-dead ancestors. Shamans serve as mediums between spirits and the living. They function in the moral order that permeates interpersonal relations and in the natural order that defines relationships between man and the earth. Angered spirit "owners" of the earth express themselves through their mediums, the shamans, who act as censors of social conduct.

Entrance into the powerful shamanistic hierarchy is controlled by the shamans themselves. Acceptance into the order is made on the basis of certain kinds of dreams that indicate the worthiness of the candidate and the genuineness of his calling by the spirits of the earth.

In these examples we can see how the dream is made to function as a vehicle of social control in many cultures.

Dreams and Social-Psychological Adjustment

The dream can be profitably studied in all cultures because it is a manifestation of the individual struggle to reconcile basic and derived needs. It is a reflection of the conflict between nature and nurture. This reflection is what David Schneider has identified as the dreamer's "definition of the situation."

Not all groups attribute great significance to the dream, nor do all groups institutionalize the dream in the service of some cultural function. The people from Tzintzuntzan, Mexico, among whom the anthropologist George M. Foster recently conducted a study of dreams, displayed largely negative attitudes toward their dreams. Tzintzuntzaños dislike discussing their dreams and sometimes disavow having them. Nevertheless, Foster maintains that his dream study was profitable in uncovering what he called large areas of the basic character and collective cognitive orientation of the people.

Thus the dream has a function even in cultures that attribute little or no significance to it, and as a consequence have not incorporated the dream into any form of institutionalized behavior. The content of the dream and what it can tell about the psychological consequences of living life in essentially different cultural environments give it an important function in all cultural settings. This is the function in which social and behavioral scientists are currently showing increased interest. This function of the dream will help us to assess psychological and other differences between peoples of different cultures. Because of this universal function of the dream, the anthropologist or psychologist can use dream data in cross-cultural investigations, even when the cultures, themselves, do not attribute any particular significance or function to the dream.

There is nothing mechanical or simple about approaches to cross-cultural dream studies. Dorothy Eggan and other dream investigators have pointed to some of the theoretical and methodological difficulties which we can expect to find in the implementation of such studies.

One of the more obvious problems, which Roy D'Andrade has brought forward, lies in the fairly obvious fact that the manifest content of the dream is not simply and directly representational of the culture from which it originates. The reason it is not appears to be that the dream is not simply a cognitive act; rather, it seems to be primarily a motivational act that generates conflict between unlearned and learned needs and desires. Nevertheless, the dream becomes cognitive in that it represents an attempt at the solution of the motivational conflict. The elements in the conflict become cognitively defined. The process of dreaming seems to be the process of laying out the nature and dimensions of the conflict and a proposal for solution.

EPILOGUE

We are taunted by the words of the English poet Samuel Taylor Coleridge: "What if you slept, and what if in your sleep you dreamed, and what if in your dream you went to heaven and there you plucked a strange and beautiful flower, and what if when you awoke you had the flower in your hand? Ah, what then?"

Poet or not, man has already plucked flowers from his dreams. Evidence for this is found in his myriad cultural and personal uses of the dream. Whatever else it might have been over the long course of human history, the flower of the dream has expressed itself in human creativity. Man has enriched himself through his dream experience. And the creativity of the dream has by no means been limited to preliterate cultures or non-Western civilizations, even though Western cultures on the whole have paid little attention to it.

We do not have to range far to find examples of dream creativity in Western cultures. "The Divine Comedy" of Dante is attributed to dream inspiration. The great German poet and dramatist Johann Wolfgang von Goethe felt that he wrote some of his best work under the inspiration of dreamlike experiences. Robert Louis Stevenson used his dream experiences extensively as a source and guide for the development of his literary material. So much did Stevenson rely upon his dreams that he attributed authorship more to his dream self than to his waking self. The poet Samuel Taylor Coleridge attributed to dream states the production of many of his works, including his poem "Kubla Khan."

But dream inspiration has also been important in other than literary fields. The philosopher Descartes, the political theorist Condorcet, the Assyriologist Hilprecht, the chemist Kekule, the physiologist Cannon, and the atomic physicist Bohr are some of the more notable in a potentially very long list of people who have made remarkable contributions to the store of human knowledge on the basis of their dreams.

At present, we find man attempting more seriously than ever before to pluck the flower of the scientific understanding of the dream. This book has been a short excursion into the world of dreams. We have had an opportunity to explore dreams from various cultural and psychological perspectives. We have been able to glimpse, however briefly, some of the more important approaches taken to reach an understanding of the *what* and *why* of the dream, and especially we have seen how, through culture, man has often been able to utilize dreams to his benefit.

In our excursion we have found that a basically scientific approach to dream understanding is just now beginning to gain momentum. What it will produce over the coming decades is naturally difficult to predict. Great strides have been made in a comparatively few years in understanding the neuro-physiological basis for dreaming. One might hope that equally great strides will be made in the behavioral and cultural understanding of the dream. When the dream has been accorded the scientific attention it deserves, man will find that he is learning things about himself that he might not be able to learn in any other way.

As G. G. Luce and J. Segal indicate in their book *Sleep*, it is highly probable that future generations in our culture will be astonished to hear of us that we could not relax, sleep, awaken, or dream at will. Be that as it may, it is quite probable that they will be astonished to find out that we were not vigorously engaged in the scientific study of the dream, such a fertile field of information.

To paraphrase Robert Van de Castle, if our predecessors in science had been more attentive to the leads available to them in the existing literature, we would not have had to wait so long for the development of the exciting new era in the biology of dreaming. If we, ourselves, attend to the signs available to us concerning the scientific importance of the dream, our descendants will probably not have to wait so long for a new psychology and anthropology of dreaming. Let us hope that these are on their way.

BIBLIOGRAPHICAL ESSAY

Dreams in the Context of Sleep and Related States

One of the least technical of the several books in this area of interest is the one by Gay Gaer Luce and Julius Segal, *Sleep* (New York: Coward, McCann and Geoghegan, 1966). Other important contributions are those of David Foulkes, *The Psychology of Sleep* (New York: Charles Scribner's Sons, 1966), and Ian Oswald, *Sleep* (Baltimore: Penguin Books, 1966). Another book of interest is that by Ernest Hartmann, *The Biology of Dreaming* (Springfield, Ill.: Charles C. Thomas, 1967).

There are numerous articles in this area of interest, only a few of which are mentioned here. One of the least technical of these is one by Ralph J. Berger, "Morpheus Descending" (*Psychology Today*, v. 4, 33-36, 70, 1970). The following are some pioneer articles discussing early research findings on physiological measures of the dream state: Eugene Aserinsky and Nathaniel Kleitman, "Regularly Occurring Periods of Eye Motility and Concomitant Phenomena During Sleep" (*Science*, v. 118, 273-274, 1953); William Dement and Nathaniel Kleitman, "Cyclic Variations in EEG During Sleep and Their Relation to Eye Movements, Body Motility, and Dreaming" (*Electroencephalography and Clinical Neurophysiology*, v. 9, 673-690, 1957); Donald R. Goodenough *et al.*, "A Comparison of 'Dreamers' and 'Non-dreamers': Eye Movements, Electroencephalograms, and the Recall of Dreams" (*Journal of Abnormal and Social Psychology*, v. 59, 295-302, 1959).

The effects of presleep and sleep stimuli are dealt with in the following works: Allan Rechtschaffen and David Foulkes, "Effects of Visual Stimuli on Dream Content" (*Perceptual and Motor Skills*, v. 20, 1149-1160, 1965). More generalized approaches to the experimental control of dreaming are

72

handled by Herman A. Witkin and Helen B. Lewis (eds.) in their *Experimental Studies of Dreaming* (New York: Random House, 1967), and by Charles T. Tart in his article, "Toward the Experimental Control of Dreaming," in the book edited by Charles T. Tart, *Altered States of Consciousness* (New York: John Wiley and Sons, 133-144, 1969).

Articles of interest on the phenomenon of narcolepsy are those by Gerald Vogel, "Studies in the Psychophysiology of Dreams: II The Dream of Narcolepsy" (*Archives of General Psychiatry*, v. 3, 421, 1960), and Allan Rechtschaffen *et al.*, "Nocturnal Sleep of Narcoleptics" (*Electroencephalography and Clinical Neurophysiology*, v. 15, 599-609, 1963).

Laboratory or experimental effects of hunger or thirst on dream content are dealt with in the following publications: F. G. Benedict *et al.*, *Human Vitality and Efficiency Under Prolonged Restriction Diet* (Washington, D.C.: Carnegie Institute Publication no. 280, 1919); Ancel Keys *et al.*, *The Biology of Human Starvation*, v. II (Minneapolis: University of Minnesota Press, 1950); William Dement and Edward Wolpert, "The Relation of Eye Movements, Body Motility, and External Stimuli to Dream Content" (*Journal of Experimental Psychology*, v. 55, 543-553, 1958); and Edwin Bokert, "Effects of Thirst and a Meaningful Related Auditory Stimulus on Dream Reports" (New York: New York University, Unpublished Ph.D. Dissertation, 1965).

The effects of other states upon the dream are treated in the following contributions: Louis Breger *et al.*, *The Effects of Stress on Dreams* (New York: International Universities Press, 1971); Montague Ullman and Stanley Krippner, *Dream Studies and Telepathy* (New York: Parapsychology Foundation, 1970); C. Scott Moss (ed.), *The Hypnotic Investigation of Dreams* (New York: John Wiley and Sons, 1970).

Articles relating the dream to other states are the following: Rosalind Cartwright, "Dreams and Drug Induced Fantasy Behavior" (*Archives of General Psychiatry*, v. 15, 7-15, 1966); Rosalind Cartwright *et al.*, "Effects of an Erotic Movie on the Sleep and Dreams of Young Men" (*Archives of General Psychiatry*, v. 20, 262-271, 1969); and Allen Dittmann and Harvey Moore, "Disturbances in Dreams as Related to Peyotism Among the Navajo" (*American Anthropologist*, v. 59, 642-649, 1957).

The important question of learning in sleep has been approached by Charles Simon and William Emmons in two informative articles, "Learning During Sleep?" (*Psychological Bulletin*, v. 52, 328-342, 1955); and "Responses to Material Presented During Various Levels of Sleep" (*The Journal of Experimental Psychology*, v. 51, 89-97, 1956).

The interesting question of how culture might influence sleep and dream cycles has been approached by John Taub, "The Sleep-Wakefulness Cycle in Mexican Adults" (*Journal of Cross-Cultural Psychology*, v. 2, 353-362, 1971).

Finally, concerning the important question of how sleep and the dream are related to wakefulness we have the contributions of Laverne Johnson, "Are Stages of Sleep Related to Waking Behavior?" (*American Scientist*, v. 61, 326-338, 1973); and Ernest Hartmann, *The Functions of Sleep* (New Haven: Yale University Press, 1973).

Dream Theories

The most important statement on psychoanalytic dream theory is that by Sigmund Freud in his 1896 book entitled *The Interpretation of Dreams* (New York: Basic Books, 1955). Also by Freud is the abbreviated statement in the book *On Dreams*, first published in 1901 (New York: W. W. Norton, 1951).

Carl Gustav Jung's theory on dreams has been dealt with in a great number of volumes by that prolific writer. Three of his works are recommended here: *Memories, Dreams and Reflections* (New York: Random House, 1961); *Modern Man in Search of a Soul* (especially Chapter 1) (New York: Harcourt, Brace, and World, 1960); *Man and His Symbols* (London: Aldus Books, 1964). The third book mentioned, *Man and His Symbols,* is perhaps his most comprehensive statement on the importance of symbols in human life, and the significance of symbols in dreams. The work was inspired by one of Jung's own dreams. A paperbound edition of this book has been published (New York: Dell Publications, Laurel edition, 1964). *Memories, Dreams and Reflections* deals in part with some of Jung's own dreams and his interpretation of the significance of these dreams in his own life experience. This book is also found in a paperback edition (New York: Alfred A. Knopf, Vintage Books, 1961).

A book by J. A. Hadfield, *Dreams and Nightmares* (Baltimore: Penguin Books, 1954), also is of important theoretical interest, as is the book by Erich Fromm, *The Forgotten Language* (New York: Grove Press, 1957). Fromm's book was first published by Rinehart, New York, in 1951. Both volumes mentioned here are in paperback editions from the presses indicated.

One of Alfred Adler's most important statements was in his article "On the Interpretation of Dreams" (*International Journal of Individual Psychology*, v. 1, 3-16, 1936). A Gestaltist understanding of the dream is dealt with in the book by Frederick Perls *et al.*, *Gestalt Therapy: Excitement and Growth in the Human Personality* (New York: Julian Press, 1969). A cognitive approach to dreams is espoused by Calvin S. Hall in "A Cognitive Theory of Dreams" (*Journal of General Psychology*, v. 49, 272-283, 1953).

Good discussions of psychological dream theories in the light of biological findings are dealt with in Part One of Milton Kramer (ed.), *Dream Psychology and the New Biology of Dreaming* (Springfield, Ill.: Charles C. Thomas, 1969). Creative aspects of the dream in relation to personality development are explored in Ernest Rossi's book, *Dreams and the Growth of Personality* (Elmsford, New York: Pergamon Press, 1972).

Assessments of empirical studies relating primarily to Freudian theories of fantasy production and dreams are treated in the following works: Seymore Feshback, "The Drive-Reducing Function of Fantasy Behavior" (*Journal of Abnormal and Social Psychology*, v. 50, 3-11, 1955); David Foulkes, "Theories of Dream Formation and Recent Studies of Sleep Consciousness" (*Psychological Bulletin*, v. 62, 236-246, 1964); and Louis Breger, "Function of Dreams" (*Journal of Abnormal Psychology Monograph*, v. 72, No. 641, 1967).

Dream theories and their implications for the social sciences are dealt with in the following contributions: Montague Ullman, "The Social Roots of the Dream" (*American Journal of Psychoanalysis*, v. 20, 180-196, 1960); Roger Bastide, "The Sociology of the Dream," in *The Dream and Human Societies*, G. E. von Grunebaum and Roger Caillois (eds.) (Berkeley: University of California Press, 199-211, 1966); Dorothy Eggan, "Dream Analysis," in *Studying Personality Cross-Culturally*, Bert Kaplan (ed.) (Evanston, Ill.: Row, Peterson, 551-577, 1961); Roy D'Andrade, "Anthropological Studies of Dreams," in *Psychological Anthropology*, Francis L. K. Hsu (ed.) (Homewood, Ill.: Dorsey Press, 296-332, 1961); and Erika Bourguignon, "Dreams and Altered States of Consciousness in Anthropological Research," in *Psychological Anthropology*, new edition, Francis L. K. Hsu (ed.) (Cambridge, Mass.: Schenkman Publishing Company, 403-434, 1971).

Different methodological approaches relating to differences in dream theories are treated in the following contributions: Jack Gershberg, "The Use of Dreams in Reality Testing" (*Comprehensive Psychiatry*, v. 10, 391-397, 1969); Thomas French and Erika Fromm, *Dream Interpretation* (New York: Basic Books, 1964); Edith Sheppard, "Systematic Dream Studies: Clinical Judgment and Objective Measurement of Ego Strength" (*Comprehensive Psychiatry*, v. 4, 263-270, 1963); Calvin S. Hall and Robert L. Van de Castle, *The Content Analysis of Dreams* (New York: Appleton-Century-Crofts, 1966); Michael Maccoby and George Foster, "Methods of Studying Mexican Peasant Personality: Rorschach, TAT and Dreams" (*Anthropological Quarterly*, v. 43, 225-242, 1970); C. Scott Moss, *Dreams, Images and Fantasy: A Semantic Differential Casebook* (Urbana, Ill.: University of Illinois Press, 1970).

In conclusion of this section, the book *Dreaming* (New York: Humanities Press, 1962) by Norman Malcolm is recommended because it challenges from a philosophical point of view some commonly held concepts of the nature of the dream which stand as assumptions in many dream theories.

Psychology of the Dream

The following books are of interest on the psychology of dreaming: Robert L. Van de Castle, *The Psychology of Dreaming* (New York: General

Learning Corporation, 1971); Richard M. Jones, *Ego Synthesis in Dreams* (Cambridge, Mass.: Schenkman Publishing Company, 1962); also by Jones, *The New Psychology of Dreaming* (New York: Grune and Stratton, 1970).

Some articles in this area of interest are those by Gardner Murphy, "The Dreamer," in *Dreams and Personality Dynamics*, Manfred F. DeMartino (ed.) (Springfield, Ill.: Charles C. Thomas, 10-29, 1959), and Erik H. Erikson, "The Dream Specimen in Psychoanalysis," in *Psychoanalytic Psychiatry and Psychology*, R. Knight and C. Friedman (eds.) (New York: International Universities Press, 131-170, 1954).

Sex- and age-related differences are dealt with in the following books and articles: Robert L. Van de Castle, "His, Hers and the Children's" (*Psychology Today*, v. 4, 37-39, 1970); Calvin S. Hall and Bill Domhoff, "An Ubiquitous Sex Difference in Dreams" (*Journal of Abnormal and Social Psychology*, v. 66, 278-280, 1963); again, the preceding authors, "Aggression in Dreams" (*International Journal of Social Psychiatry*, v. 9, 259-267, 1963); A. F. Paolino, "Dreams: Sex Differences in Aggressive Content" (*Journal of Projective Techniques and Personality Assessment*, v. 28, 219-226, 1964); Kenneth M. Colby, "Sex Differences in Dreams in Primitive Tribes" (*American Anthropologist*, v. 65, 1116-1122, 1963); Phyllis Booth, "Sex Differences in the Content of South African Dreams" (Chicago: University of Chicago, Unpublished M.A. Thesis, 1966); Michael Robbins and Philip Kilbride, "Sex Differences in Dreams in Uganda" (*Journal of Cross-Cultural Psychology*, v. 2, 406-408, 1971).

The following relate more specifically to the study of children's dreams: Arthur J. Jersild *et al.*, *Children's Fears, Dreams, Wishes, Daydreams, Likes, Dislikes, Pleasant and Unpleasant Memories* (New York: Columbia University Press, 1933); Charles W. Kimmins, *Children's Dreams* (New York: Longmans, Green and Company, 1920); Jean Piaget, *Play, Dreams and Imitation in Childhood* (New York: W. W. Norton, 1962); Lawrence Kohlberg, "Cognitive States and Pre-school Education" (*Human Development*, v. 9, 5-17, 1966); Barbara Lloyd and Richard Light, "Cognitive Stages in Dream Concept Development in English Children" (*Journal of Social Psychology*, v. 82, 271-272, 1970); David Foulkes *et al.*, "Two Studies of Childhood Dreaming" (*American Journal of Orthopsychiatry*, v. 39, 627-643, 1969).

Generalized sex-related differences are dealt with in Brooks Brenneis, "Male and Female Ego Modalities in Manifest Dream Content" (*Journal of Abnormal Psychology*, v. 76, 434-442, 1970); and in an earlier work by M. Friedmann, "Representative and Typical Dreams with Emphasis on the Masculinity-Femininity Problem" (*Psychoanalytic Review*, v. 44, 363-389, 1957).

Some effects of sleep and dream deprivation are dealt with in the following articles: E. Murray *et al.*, "The Effects of Sleep Deprivation on Social

Behavior" (*Journal of Social Psychology*, v. 49, 229, 1959); William Dement, "The Effect of Dream Deprivation" (*Science*, v. 131, 1705-1707, 1960); Ralph J. Berger and Ian Oswald, "Effects of Sleep Deprivation on Behavior, Subsequent Sleep, and Dreaming" (*Journal of Mental Science*, v. 108, 455-465, 1962); Charles Fisher and William Dement, "Studies on the Psychopathology of Sleep and Dreams" (*American Journal of Psychiatry*, v. 119, 1160, 1963).

Cultural, Cross-Cultural, and Historical Dream Studies

A general work on the history of dreams in literate cultures is Raymond De Becker, *The Understanding of Dreams and Their Influence on the History of Man* (New York: Hawthorn Books, 1968). A general work dealing with the significance of the dream in preliterate cultures is Jackson Steward Lincoln, *The Dream in Primitive Cultures* (Baltimore: The Williams and Wilkins Company, 1935); out of print for many years, this classic Lincoln study has been reprinted by Johnson Reprint Corporation, New York and London, 1970.

The dream is treated as a central area of interest in the following books: George Devereux shows how he used dreams to psychoanalyze a "Wolf" Indian and also learn about "Wolf" culture in *Reality and Dream* (Garden City, N.Y.: Doubleday, 1969). Robert A. LeVine does a cross-cultural analysis of dreams from three cultures in Nigeria, relating his findings to important social structural variables in *Dreams and Deeds* (Chicago: University of Chicago Press, 1966). Géza Róheim treats culture as a projection of the dream in *The Eternal Ones of the Dream* (New York: International Universities Press, 1945), and in *The Gates of the Dream* (same press, 1952). David Schneider and Lauriston Sharp present us with an analysis of selected manifest elements in the dreams of the Yir Yoront of Australia in *The Dream Life of a Primitive People* (Ann Arbor: University Microfilms, 1969). Kilton Stewart analyzes the psychological and cultural implications of dreams for Negritos and other cultural groups in the Philippines in *Pygmies and Dream Giants* (New York: W. W. Norton, 1954). G. E. von Grunebaum and Roger Caillois (eds.) have compiled a number of interesting and worthwhile contributions on the dream from scholars in various disciplines who participated in the international colloquium on the dream held in France in 1962. Their book is entitled *The Dream and Human Societies* (Berkeley: University of California Press, 1966).

Frequently in anthropological literature the dream is treated as a subject of only incidental interest. Some examples are the following: Allan Holmberg, *Nomads of the Long Bow: The Sirionó of Eastern Bolivia* (New York: Natural History Press, 1969); Alfred L. Kroeber, "Ethnographic Interpretations: 2 Ad Hoc Reassurance Dreams" *University of California Publications in American Archaeology and Ethnology*, v. 47, 205-208, 1937); and I. M.

Lewis, *Ecstatic Religion: An Anthropological Study of Spirit Possession and Shamanism* (Baltimore: Penguin Books, 1971).

Some interesting articles dealing with the cultural and social meaning and use of dreams are the following: Kilton Stewart discusses the significance and use of dreams by the Senoi of Malaya in "Dream Theory in Malaya," to be found in Charles T. Tart (ed.), *Altered States of Consciousness* (New York: John Wiley and Sons, 159-167, 1969). Raymond Firth deals with the importance of dreams among the Tikopians in "The Meaning of Dreams in Tikopia," in the volume *Essays Presented to Charles Gabriel Seligman*, edited by E. Evans-Pritchard, R. Firth, B. Malinowski, and I. Schapera (London; Kegan Paul, 63-74, 1934). A. Irving Hallowell deals with "The Role of Dreams in Ojibwa Culture" in *The Dream and Human Societies*, G. E. von Grunebaum and Roger Caillois (eds.) (Berkeley: University of California Press, 267-292, 1966). Clyde Kluckhohn and William Morgan discuss the significance of Navajo dreams in "Some Notes on Navajo Dreams" in W. Muensterberger (ed.), *Essays in Honor of Géza Róheim* (New York: International Universities Press, 120-131, 1951).

Among some of the earlier studies concerning cultural uses of the dream we have: In R. Keable's article, "A People of Dreams" (*The Hibbert Journal*, April, 522-531, 1921), he illustrates how the Basuto use dreams to justify certain actions. In Robert H. Lowie's "The Religion of the Crow Indians" (*Anthropological Papers of the American Museum of Natural History*, v. 25, 317, 323-324, 1922), he deals with the ritual significance of the dream vision. Ruth Benedict indicates the place of the vision and the dream in the guardian-spirit complex in "The Concept of the Guardian Spirit in North America" (*Memoirs of the American Anthropological Association*, v. 29, 1923). A paper by Willard Z. Park, "Paviotso Shamanism" (*American Anthropologist*, v. 36, 99, 1934), describes how shamans among the Paviotso are "called" to their status through dreams. A contribution by Paul Radin discusses "Some Aspects of Puberty Fasting Among the Ojibwa" (*Canada, Department of Mines Museum Bulletin no. 2*, Ottawa, 1914).

Somewhat more recent studies on the cultural uses of the dream are the following: The great importance of the dream in Mojave culture is dealt with by W. J. Wallace, "The Dream in Mojave Life" (*Journal of American Folklore*, v. 60, 252-258, 1947). Also treating the significance of the dream in Mojave culture, George Devereux wrote "Dream Learning and Individual Ritual Differences in Mojave Shamanism" (*American Anthropologist*, v. 59, 1039-1045, 1957). Comparing psychoanalytic and Iroquoian dream theories, Anthony F. C. Wallace wrote "Dreams and the Wishes of the Soul: A Type of Psychoanalytic Theory Among the Seventeenth-Century Iroquois" (*American Anthropologist*, v. 60, 234-248, 1958). Illustrating the dream as a mechanism to reinforce social values, Mervyn J. Meggitt wrote "Dream

Interpretation Among the Mae Enga of New Guinea" (*Southwestern Journal of Anthropology*, v. 18, 216-229, 1962).

Some articles have pointed out mutual influences between culture and the dream. One such article is that by S. G. Lee, "Social Influences in Zulu Dreaming," found in *Cross-Cultural Studies*, edited by Douglass Price-Williams (Baltimore: Penguin Books, 307-328, 1970). Another article, by George Devereux, also points to the two-way influence between culture and dream: "Pathogenic Dreams in Non-Western Societies" in G. E. von Grunebaum and Roger Caillois (eds.) *The Dream and Human Societies* (Berkeley: University of California Press, 213-228, 1966).

A number of authors have written on anthropological approaches to dream research. One such contribution, illustrating a long-term investment in field research, is that by John J. Honigmann, "The Interpretation of Dreams in Anthropological Field Work" in Bert Kaplan (ed.), *Studying Personality Cross-Culturally* (Evanston, Ill.: Row, Peterson, 579-585, 1961). Dorothy Eggan has written some articles on the subject: "The Significance of Dreams for Anthropological Research" (*American Anthropologist*, v. 51, 177-198, 1949); and "The Manifest Content of Dreams: A Challenge to Social Science" (*American Anthropologist*, v. 54, 469-485, 1952).

Focusing on manifest dream elements, Richard Griffith *et al.* analyzed similarities and differences in the dreams of college students in Japan and in the United States in "The University of Typical Dreams" (*American Anthropologist*, v. 60, 1173-1179, 1958). Using the same basic approach, Z. Giora *et al.* analyzed the dreams of rural Israeli and Arab youths in "Dreams in Cross-Cultural Research" (*Comprehensive Psychiatry*, v. 13, 105-114, 1972).

Also focusing on the manifest content of dreams, Carl O'Nell studied motivational states expressed in dreams, "A Cross-Cultural Study of Hunger and Thirst Motivation Manifested in Dreams" (*Human Development*, v. 8, 181-193, 1965). He also studied sex differences in dreams in Zapotec society in "Sex Differences in Aggression in Waking Life and in Dreams in a Zapotec Community," a paper read to the Central States Anthropological Society, 1969, and in "Male and Female Dreamworlds in a Zapotec Community," a paper read to the American Anthropological Association, 1969. A study of manifest aggressive content in dreams was made by Carl O'Nell and Nancy O'Nell, comparing a Zapotec dream sample with the sample of American dreams studied by Calvin Hall and Bill Domhoff, "Aggression in Dreams" (*International Journal of Social Psychiatry*, v. 9, 259-267, 1963); their article (in press), "A Cross-Cultural Comparison of Aggression in Dreams: Zapotecs and Americans" will appear in the *International Journal of Social Psychiatry*.

Some recent and interesting analyses of manifest content appear in these studies: Robert L. Munroe *et al.*, "Effects of Population Density on Food

Concerns in Three East African Societies" (*Journal of Health and Social Behavior*, v. 10, 161-171, 1969). Alan Krohn and David Gutmann, "Changes in Mastery Style with Age"—a study of the Navajo (*Psychiatry*, v. 34, 289-300, 1971). George M. Foster, "Dreams, Character, and Cognitive Orientation in Tzintzuntzan" (*Ethos*, v. 1, 106-121, 1973).

Works of General Interest

A very readable book of perennial interest, stressing the importance of the manifest dream, is that by Calvin S. Hall, *The Meaning of Dreams* (New York: Dell Publishing Company, 1959).

For those interested in the religious significance of the dream, there are Morton T. Kelsey's *Dreams: The Dark Speech of the Spirit* (Garden City, N.Y.: Doubleday, 1968); and John A. Sanford's *Dreams: God's Forgotten Language* (Philadelphia: J. B. Lippincott, 1968).

A work of general interest, well written and beautifully illustrated, is the book by Norman MacKenzie, *Dreams and Dreaming* (New York: Vanguard Press, 1965). A recent anthology presenting contributions on the dream from authors in many walks of life and from ancient times to the present is the book edited by Ralph Woods and Herbert Greenhouse, *The New World of Dreams* (New York: Macmillan, 1974).

For people who wish to use their dreams for greater self-knowledge, there are three volumes which are of interest: Ann Faraday has written two of them, *Dream Power* (New York): Coward, McCann and Geoghegan, 1972) and *The Dream Game* (New York: Harper and Row, 1974). The third book is by Calvin S. Hall and Vernon J. Nordby, *The Individual and His Dreams* (New York: New American Library, 1972).

For people who would like to remember their dreams better, there are two short but informative articles related to that topic. One of these is by Margie Casady, "Dream Catching: A Few Easy Steps to Remembering Dreams"; the other is by David Cohen, "To Sleep, Perchance to Recall a Dream." Both are found in *Psychology Today*, v. 7, 50-54, 1974.

And, finally, for those who might like to read dreams reported for the famous and infamous, there is an anthology compiled by Brian Hill, *Gates of Horn and Ivory* (New York: Taplinger, 1968).

INDEX